Lokmanya Bal Gangadhar Tilak

Lokmanya Bal Gangadhar Tilak

Dr. Jitendra Rana

Akashdeep Publications
New Delhi-110030

Lokmanya Bal Gangadhar Tilak

First Edition : 2019

ISBN : 978-81-944528-3-6

Price : ₹ 895/-

Published by

Akashdeep Publications

1/1079E, Mehrauli
New Delhi-110030

PRINTED IN INDIA

Contents

Preface

Bal Gangadhar Tilak (July 23, 1856-August 1, 1920), was an Indian nationalist, social reformer and freedom fighter who was the first popular leader of the Indian Independence Movement and is known as "Father of the Indian unrest."

An assessment of Tilak's role in the Freedom Movement has often been hampered by charges of "communalism" and "Hindu Revivalism". But a closer and more balanced inspection of Tilak's record in public life reveals a rather different picture. As early as 1888, Tilak had made a decisive break with his former cohort-Chiplunkar, unwilling to align with any narrow and sectarian agenda of chauvinist Hindu revivalism. This is not to say that Tilak was indifferent to Hindu traditions. Few leaders were. Many of the Muslim leaders were Maulanas, and Hindu leaders often had connections with the Arya Samaj or Brahmo Samaj. Tilak's interest in the Gita was neither exceptional, nor should it have brought any unduly unfavorable commentaries.

His popular quote, "Swaraj is my inheritance, and I should have it!" is very much recollected in India even today. Respectfully tended to as Lokmanya (signifying "Cherished of the general population" or "Loved by the world"), Tilak was a researcher of Indian history, Sanskrit, Hinduism, science, law and space science.

Gangadhar Tilak joined the Indian National Congress in 1890. He soon started vocalizing his strong opposition to the moderate views of the party on self-rule. He maintained that simple constitutional agitation in itself was futile against the British. This subsequently made him stand against the prominent Congress leader, Gopal Krishna Gokhale. He wanted an armed revolt to broom-away the British.

Tilak created a revolution in the world of ethics with his Gitarahasya. It had far reaching consequences in the field of religion, politics, relationship with religious minorities and national struggle for independence. Below we take a critical look at his ethical views and its impact on the Hindutva ideology which is in vogue. K.M.Panikkar observes that it is Tilak's Gitarahasya which marked the change in Indian political scenario. He showed for the first time that the message of the Gita was not renunciation as others had thought before, but it was essentially a scripture preaching a doctrine of social activism where action for human good without personal attachment is preached as the first imperative.

Partition of Bengal created a massive outburst of public anger against British rule. Intellectual people as well as common man took part in mass agitation. Poet Rabindranath Tagore actively supported the movement. Bankim Chandra Chatterjee's 'Bande Matram' was taken up as the soul-stirring slogan. Several groups of revolutionaries started operating in Bengal. Aurobindo Ghosh (later known as Sri Aurobindo), Rasbihari Bose and Jatindranath Mukherjee (Bagha Jatin) were some of the important leaders of these revolutionary groups.

This is a reference book. All the matter is just compiled and edited in nature, taken from the various sources which are in public domain.

The book will prove an informative and most useful asset for students, scholars and teachers in this field. The book is of great importance for the scholars, researchers, students, teachers and historians as well pertaining to this sphere.

—Editor

1

Biography

Bal Gangadhar Tilak (July 23, 1856-August 1, 1920), was an Indian patriot, social reformer and opportunity warrior who was the principal mainstream pioneer of the Indian Independence Movement and is known as "Father of the Indian turmoil."

Tilak was one of the first and most grounded advocates for Swaraj (finish autonomy) in Indian cognizance, and is viewed as the father of Hindu patriotism too.

His popular quote, "Swaraj is my inheritance, and I should have it!" is very much recollected in India even today. Respectfully tended to as Lokmanya (signifying "Cherished of the general population" or "Loved by the world"), Tilak was a researcher of Indian history, Sanskrit, Hinduism, science, law and space science.

EARLY LIFE

Tilak was born in *Madhali Alee* (Middle Lane) in Ratnagiri, Maharashtra, into a middle class family. He graduated from Deccan College, Pune in 1877.

After graduation, Tilak began teaching mathematics in a private school in Pune and later became a journalist. He became a strong critic of the Western education system, feeling it demeaned the Indian students and disrespected India's heritage. He organized the Deccan Education Society to improve the quality of education for India's youth. He taught Mathematics at Fergusson College.

TILAK'S THEORY IS BASED ESSENTIALLY ON THE ASTRONOMICAL EVIDENCE

He states, "We find that the Rigveda hymns had already become antiquated and unintelligible in the days of the Taittiriya Samhita and the Brahmans. The Taittiriya Samhita places the vernal equinox in the Krittikas, and I have shown that we must fix its date at about 2500 B.C. If the hymns of the Rigveda were unintelligible at this time, they must have been sung several centuries before it."

The expression "I am Margasirsa among months" attracted Tilak's attention because he saw in it some clue to the Vedic chronology for the simple reason that the names of months in the Hindu calendar are derived from the names of nakshatras. Presently our new year starts from Chaitra, but as Whitney has shown, it began in Margasirsa according to the Surya Siddhanta. Sacrifice (yajna) is the base of the Vedic culture, and is closer, related to the Sun. Hence, for the performance of sacrifice a good knowledge of months, seasons and sun's movements was essential. Everyday the Nakshatra close to the sun was noted, and the time it took to come to the same position was counted as one year. The beginning of the year was the commencement of the sacrifice and it (Satra) continued for tile whole year. According to the Vedanga-Jyotisha, new year starts from winter. This is known as the vernal equinox (Uttaryana), which means the sun's movement from the south to the north. It has been observed that the seasons lag behind by one month after every two thousand years, and this change has to be adjusted in the calendar. This can be proved by the statement that "the sun is in the asterism of Krittikas," which occurs in the Taittiriya Samhita.

The equinoxes are the two days of the year when the Sun is directly above the equator. As the earth moves in its orbit around the sun, the position of the sun changes in relation to the equator. The sun appears north of the equator between the March equinox and the September equinox. It Is south of the equator between the September equinox and the next March equinox.

This happened in 2350 B.C. With this as a fixed datum, the various stages of the Vedic literature have been dated by Tilak.

According to him, the oldest Vedic calendar, the oldest Vedic hymn, was sacrificial, and therefore the sacrifice of the year commenced with Aditi at the vernal equinox in or near Punarvasu. The tradition about the old beginnings of the year is mentioned in the Taittiriya Samhita, and the same is corroborated by the oldest traditions and records of the Parsis and the Greeks who also belonged to the Aryan race. On the basis of the evidence furnished by astronomical references in the Taittiriya Sanhita Tilak developed his chronology for the Vedic literature as follows.

I. *The Oldest Period*: The oldest period in the Aryan civilization which may be called Aditi or the Pre-Orion period which, according to Tilak, can be provided 6000-4000 BC time bracket. He observes that the Parsis and the Greeks who, though belonging to the Aryan race, have not retained the tradition of this period because "they carried with them the calendar which was in force when they left the common home, while the Indian Aryans have preserved all the traditions with a super religious fidelity and scrupulousness."

II. *The Orion Period (4000-2500 B.C.)* : This period starts from the time when the vernal equinox was in the asterism of Ardra (Orion) and continues upto the time when it receded to the asterism of the Krittikas. This, according to Tilak, was the most important period in the development of the Aryan civilization. It was pre-eminently the period of the hymns which contain a record of the beginning of the year when several legends were conceived. (*e.g.* the legend of Vrisakapi).

III. *The Krittika Period (2500-1400 B.C.)* : This period begins when the vernal equinox was in the asterism of the Krittikas and continues upto the period recorded in the Vedanga Jyotish. It was the period of the Taittiriya Samhita and many of the Brahmans were composed during this period. According to Tilak, "The hymns of the Rigveda had already become unique and unintelligible by this time and the Brahmavadins engaged in speculations about the real meaning of these hymns and legends."

IV. Pre-Buddhist period (1400-500 B.C.) : This was the period when the Sutra literature was composed.

Tilak concludes his theory with the following statement:

"The astronomical method, I admit, is vague in so far as it does not enable us to determine the exact date of all the Vedic hymns or works, but it is certainly superior to linguistic method inasmuch as it supplies us with certain definite, undisputed facts, for instance, the position of the equinoxes, which can safely be made the nuclei of the different periods of antiquity."

He further adds "thus we find that of all the ancient nations the Hindus alone had well nigh accurately determined the rate of the motion of the procession of the equinoxes."

Tilak records his debt to the Late Professor R. G. Bhandarkar, his teacher at Deccan College, Pune, for explaining to him the views of certain German scholars and Khan Bahadur Dr. Dastur Hoshang Jamasp for Parsee traditions.

In the Orion Tilak has given quite a new and convincing interpretation of some eighty verses in the Rigveda besides shedding a welcome light on many more. These verses had baffled the students of Vedic literature for long even from the time of Sayanacharya. His theory of 'cosmic circulation of aerial waters' properly explained the Indra-Vrtra myth.

Tilak's dating of the Vedas to such an early period in the fourth millennium was not acceptable to a majority of western scholars, as for instance, Max Mueller who was not prepared to go beyond the second millennium B.C. although he had at one stage concluded that it is impossible to determine the date of the Vedic literature and that it may be four thousand or five thousand year old. But there were quite a few who agreed with Tilak. Professor Hermann Jacobi had simultaneously, but independently, arrived at the conclusion that the antiquity of the Vedas can go back to 6000 B.C. Dr. Bloomfield, an eminent American scholar, was sceptical at first but, as he read through, he was inclined to agree with Tilak's views. He confessed that he was convinced in all essential points and that the book was unquestionably the literary sensation of the year.

It will be interesting to examine Tilak's theory in the light of recent archaeological research. Hundred years have passed since Tilak expounded his views. In his time the Indus civilization had not been discovered; but now we know it in all its glory. It must be stated that there are quite a few who identify it as the civilization of the Vedic Aryans although the general opinion seems to assign it to a post-Harappan date in the later half of the second millennium B.C. It may not be out of place to mention here that the recent archaeological data have not yielded any evidence for the Aryan invasion. Moreover, the beginning of the settled life in the Indian subcontinent now goes back to almost ten thousand years as is clear from the excavation at Mehragh which is located at the mouth of the Bolan Pass near Quetta in Pakistan.

The excavated evidence points to continuous habitation starting from 7500 B.C. and ending around 3000 B.C. which marks the Early Harappan phase out of which evolved the Indus or the Harappan civilization. The only noticeable culture change in all the four and a half millennia of continuous habitation is between 6000 B.C. to 4500 B. C. which indicates the arrival of a new group of people or new cultural influences. These are precisely the dates that Tilak has assigned to his Pre-Orion period. This may be sheer coincidence and it will not be prudent to read too much into it at this stage, but at the same time it cannot be dismissed out of hand.

The Bhagwad-Gita

Tilak is known more for his Gita-Rahasya than his other scholarly works. He was once asked by his father, who was on his deathbed, to read the Gita to him. He was then a young lad of sixteen in 1872, but even at tender age was thinking as to what was really the message of the Gita. He was pondering over it and was very much interested in writing on it but could not do so because of his multifarious activities-social and political, and had therefore to postpone it every time. Finally, when he was imprisoned in 1908 in Mandalay, he requested the government to permit him to take some books with him. It was granted and he has noted in the Preface to the Gita Rahasya that in the winter of 1910-11, he wrote out the first draft, made improvements as and when possible, but since he had not with him the required reference books, he finally completed the work during his sojourn at Sinhagad near Pune. Even then he felt that it was not as thorough and complete in all respects as he desired. He was dictating it to his assistant, some 10-12 pages a day, and the latter wrote in long hand as it was in Marathi. He wrote it in four months and published it in June 1915.

Among the ancient commentaries on the Gita, only that by Shankaracharya is available, and it is highly likely that there were others also. It is well known that the Prasthana-trayi consisting of the Upanisads the Brahma-Sutras and the Gita-constitutes the foundation of the philosophy of Hinduism. Sankaracharya advocated advaita, and preached that only sanyasa leads to the final salvation (moksa). Tilak, on the other hand argues that the Gita teaches us to do our duty in whatever station of life we are. The message of the Gita is thus Karma-yoga.

On the battle field, at the very commencement of the Mahabharata war, Arjuna was perplexed that the enemy were his own kith and kin, and was in two minds whether he should fight or not. Hence Krishna, who was also his charioteer, had to impress upon him that he should do his duty, that is to fight. What the Lord emphasizes is that one should do his ordained duty and while performing it, one should not expect any fruit. This is the niskam-karma-yoga of the Gita. In the Gita Tilak found that the cult of sacrifice was replaced by that of Bhakti, and that it gave the message of karma-yoga and not that of sanyasa as propounded by Sankaracharya.

The Gita Rahasya received numerous accolades from different quarters but the most telling was the praise showered by Sri Aurobindo who found the work "an original criticism and presentation of ethical monumental work, the first prose writing of the front rank in importance... and is likely to become a classic."

Tilak wrote the Gita-Rahasya in Marathi, and when his friends asked him why did he not write in English, he replied that it is not a piece of research, but was written for the common man who should imbibe the karma-yoga as interpreted by him. Moreover, he said that the people in the western world are already practicing karma-yoga and that is why they have prospered; hence they need not be taught it.

When the book was first published in 1915, the first edition of six thousand copies was sold like hot cakes, and there were queues outside the Kesari office in Gaikwad Wada. Although a vast majority of the people agreed with Tilak's interpretation of the Gita, there were some, particularly in Pune, who criticized it out of sheer jealousy. Some opposed Tilak's views because they were contradictory to those of Shankaracharya. Be that as it may, the book was immensely popular as the printing history shows, and was also translated into English and many Indian languages.

Research Papers

Besides these major research works, Lokmanya Tilak also wrote a few research papers. The most interesting amongst these is 'The Chaldean and Indian Vedas', which was originally a lecture that he delivered at the Cama Oriental Research Institute in Bombay on 6 December 1904, and was later contributed to the R. G. Bhandarkar Commemoration Volume. Interesting archaeological discoveries were being made in West Asia at the beginning of the twentieth century noteworthy among which were the inscribed tablets unearthed in large numbers in Mesopotamia which, on decipherment, were found to record what scholars have aptly refereed to as the Chaldean Veda. Tilak had come across certain nonsanskrit works in course of his study of the Atharva Veda. Since, according to him, the Vedic and the Chaldean civilization were contemporary, there must have been culture contact between them. He showed how the word 'mana' was borrowed by the Vedic. Much more interesting and ingenious, however, is the similarity in Taimata and Urugula of the Av with Tiamat and Urgala of the Accadian legends. Tilak has discussed some other words which throw light on the contacts between India and West Asia in the ancient past.

Yet another paper deals with 'A missing verse in the Sankhya Karikas'. The Sankhya Karika of Ishwarkrishna contained 70 verses, but only 69 are available. Tilak reconstructed the missing verse on the basis of the evidence of the commentary of Gaudapada. There are some more papers which have been published in a book entitled Vedic Chronology and Vedanga Jyotish. Tilak wrote a series of eight articles in the Kesari on the Mahabharata, which, though reviewed C. V. Vaidya's monumental work on the epic, are also important for his deep insight into the subject. Vaidya had dated the Mahabharata war to about 300 B.C., but Tilak has very convincingly shown that the event in all probability occurred around 1400 B.C. which date is in agreement with that proposed by a majority of scholars. Many of Tilak's editorials display his wide erudition and keen intellect. He wrote on a variety of subjects such as Ramayana, Bababhatta, Vishnu-sahasranama, Agnosticism and so on which bear eloquent testimony to his versatile genius.

All of Tilak's writings are marked by a remarkable clarity of style, forceful language—whether English or Marathi—and elegant prose. They also display his wide erudition which is at once interesting and instructive and is free from cumbersome jargon. This is obviously due to his being basically a teacher of Sanskrit and Mathematics. He was gifted with an imagination of a very high order and his genius was comprehensive and subtle.

The sheer speed with which he wrote is simply amazing. He dictated almost a dozen pages at a stretch and worked for over sixteen hours a day. This could be possible because of his super-abundant energy and robust health which he has acquired during his student days. He was a true practitioner of the Karmayoga which, according to him, was the gospel of the Gita.

The great Indian philosopher, S. Radhakrishnan wrote that "his (Tilak's) real genius lay in literacy work." His essay on `A missing verse in the Sankhya Karika' is regarded by scholars as a notable contribution to the interpretation of the Sankhya Philosophy. His Orion started the western world. Mahatma Gandhi was highly impressed by his encyclopaedic learning which he carried lightly. Had he been able to devote all his energies to study and research, he would have certainly solved many riddles of Hinduism. He was a great Indologist.

TILAK'S EQUIPMENT AS HISTORIAN

Tilak was not a professional historian. He entered into the field of historical research by sheer accident.

The initial success in the research of the antiquity of the Vedas, encouraged him to do further research and as a sequel to his Orion or Researches into the Antiquity of the Vedas, Tilak produced another original research book, 'The Arctic Home' in the Vedas' in 1898, during the period of his eighteen months imprisonment at Yervada in 1897-98. The book was, however, published in 1903, because of his busy schedule after his release from imprisonment. The main theme of his research was-where was the earliest home of the Vedas? With a view to resolve this issue he studied geological researches about the commencement of the post-glacial period, the historic evidence from the Vedic and the allied literature, the characteristics of the polar region, and produced a book entitled 'The Arctic Home in the Vedas' having 13 chapters running into 450 pages. He presented a mass of evidence to prove conclusively that before the commencement of the post-glacial epoch, the North Pole regions were inhabited by the Aryan race, and that those people migrated from this place southwards in Asia and Europe not by any 'irrestible impulse' but by unwelcome changes in the climatic conditions of their original home.

Plunge in Maratha History

However, the peculiar circumstances that were prevailing in the last decades of the 19th century, made him set aside his prime interest in the researches of Ancient India, and plunge into the history of the immediate past of Maharahstra *i.e.* the Maratha History.

The intellectuals of Maharashtra had started taking interest in their history. Neelakantha Janardhan Kirtane, a junior student of the Deccan College, assailed Grant Duff's History of the Marathas (1826) in his lecture delivered in the Young Men's Association of the College in 1868. He rhetorically pointed out that Grant's History was no more than an account of the military expeditions of the Marathas, rather than the glorious achievements of the Maratha people, of which the people of this region were proud. Rajwade V.K. another historian of the Marathas, after enlisting many deficiencies and mistakes in Grant's History confirmed the assessment of Kirtane and said further that his history was not more than a chronicle. Grant's history was also translated into Marathi by Captain David and Baba Sane and published in 1829-30. Text books on History were prepared on the basis of information contained in these histories which presented a distorted picture of the Maratha Rule with a view to justify their conquest of the country. It was, therefore, necessary to remove the prejudices developed by the non-Marathi speaking people, through reading the historical writings of the British to whom the Marathas were simply plunderers who thrived on looting other Indian powers.

The British rulers, who strove to inculcate the feeling of distrust among the Indians, and prevent the revival of Maratha power, put restrictions on the researches in the Maratha period, which was a hot bed according to them. This restrictive policy of the British denying free access to the archival material preserved in the Government Archives, induced a group of Marathi scholars to launch a popular movement for collecting historical material from the historically old families of the Marathas in the last quarter of the 19th century. Individual historians like Kashinath Narayan Sane (1851-1927) Vasudev Shastri Khare (1858-1924), Vinayak Kashinath Rajwade (1864-1926) and Dattatraya Balwant Parasnis (1870-1926) dug out private archives of Maratha princes, jagirdars, sardars, ministers, and others to counteract the restrictive policy of the colonial rule and present an authentic and real picture of the Maratha power, and remove thereby the misgivings created by the historical writing of the British. Rajwade V.K., for instance founded the Bharat Itihas Samshodhak Mandal at Pune in 1910 on the model of the German historian Leopold Von Ranke (1795-1886), with a view to collect, preserve, and publishing authentic source material and promote scientific research in Indian history. The latter half of the 19th century witnessed a flood of historical writings including various forms of literature like novels, plays, poetry, epics, miscellaneous writings, besides the publication of source material. Thus, the period from Gopal Hari Deshmukh, (Popularly known as Lokhitwadi) (1823-

1892) to Lokmanya B.G. Tilak (1856-1920) produced many historical writings, which helped to awaken the interests of masses in their past history.

Immediate Cause

However the immediate cause which aroused much interest in Shivaji among the intellectuals, elites and masses of Maharashtra was the references to the dilapidated condition of Shivaji's tomb at Raigad, made by a British visitor James Douglas in his work entitled 'A book of Bombay', first published in 1883 and reproduced in his bigger book 'Bombay and Western Indian' published from London in 1893. Douglas visited the Raigad fort in 1883 and when he found the cenotaph (Samadhi) of Shivaji in a dilapidated condition, the temple in a wretched plight, and the image therein thrown on the ground, pathetically observed, "Nobody now cares for Shivaji, not one rupee is spent on the annual repairs of the tomb of Shivaji Maharaj who was master of an enormous kingdom."

Douglas further urged the British Government, who had acquired the Kingdom of Shivaji and his successors to look into this matter, in a note in which he said, "The British Government conserves the architectural remains of Tudor and Stuarts. Will not the Bombay Government do as much for the tomb, the temple and the arch of Shivaji? A few crumbs that fall from the archaeological bureau of Western India would suffice to keep in repair memorials of a dashing and most romantic period."

The efforts of James Douglas, however, did not go in vain. In view of these remarks, and the pressure from the public, the British Government, not only declared it as a Monument of Protection but also made some provision for its repairs and maintenance.

The remarks of James Douglas about the neglect of the forts in general and Raigad in particular also created a stir in Maharashtra and both the press and the intellectuals resented the Government policy strongly. Raigad was made the symbol of patriotism, and people were reminded by the Press, as early as 1885, of their negligence of patriotism. Justice M.G. Ranade, the author of the famous classic 'Rise of the Maratha Power' organised a public meeting at Hirabag in Pune in 1886 to promote interest in the issue of Shivaji Memorial. It was attended by many important people including the Maratha Sardars, Landlords and even the representative c f the Kolhapur State.

LATER YEARS AND LEGACY

Tilak was a critic of Mahatma Gandhi's strategy of non-violence, civil disobedience. Although once considered an extremist revolutionary, in his later years Tilak had considerably mellowed. He favoured political dialogue and discussions as a more effective way to obtain political freedom for India.

When Tilak died in 1920, Gandhi paid his respects at his cremation in Bombay, along with 200,000 people. Gandhi called Tilak *"The Maker of Modern India"*. Tilak is also today considered the father of Hindu Nationalism. He was the idol of Indian revolutionary Vinayak Damodar Savarkar, who penned the political doctrine of Hindutva. He realized that the constitutional agitation in itself was futile against the British and that, moreover, India was ill prepared for an armed revolt.

As a result, although he was helpful to revolutionaries such as Savarkar, Aurobindo Ghosh and Chaphekar, he did not venture into it himself. Instead, he martialled the extremist wing of Indian National Congress. His movement was based on the principles of Swadeshi (Indigenous), Boycott and Education. It was he who, through his own example, gave prestige to imprisonment in freedom struggle. It is a tragedy that his work is not given the recognition due to it.

Tilak is often misinterpreted. Perhaps it is so because of his style of operation which raised bitter controversies and still more bitter opponenents even outside the beurocracy. Violent arguements characterized his relationship with social reformists such as Agarkar, Ranade and moderates like Ferozshah Mehta. Many blame him for opposing the Age of Consent Bill which raised the age limit for marriage of girls to 12 (from 10). But is fact that at the same time he had signed a counter-proposal where in one of the clauses was that the girls (boys) should not be married until they are 16 (20). He educated all of his daughters and did not marry them till they were over 16. There are instances when he privately paid for the education of women. Still it remains true that he was a reactionary and did not use his considerable influence to give a much-needed support to the social reformists. Probably, he did not want to offend the prevalent rigid system-he, himself, having been brought up in the culturally narrow surroundings of Pune. It seems as if his canvas presented him no room for active social reforms.

He had several discussions with Shankaracharya of Sankeshwar and asserted that like Swami Vivekananda, the modern Shankaracharya must be educated on modern lines. Tilak received Bachelor of Arts degree from The Deccan College, Pune in 1879 and L.L.B. from the Elphinston College, Mumbai in 1882.

He was among the founders of the New English School, Pune (1881) of which Prof Chiplunkar became the Principal. He had a genius for organisation and with Agarkar, the then foremost social reformist, started the newspapers 'Kesari' and 'The Maratha' in 1881 and in 1890's started the annual celebration of 'Shivaji Festival' and 'Ganapati Festival' which served a platform for people to join in the nationalist movement against the British. Soon he came to be regarded as the undisputed leader of Maharashtra and was honoured with the title 'Lokamanya' in 1893 which became synonymous with him in the 1900.

As the nation fumed over the partition of Bengal (1905), Tilak assumed the national leadership with his extremist attitude and stated his position unequivocally as "Swarajya (self rule) is my birth right and I shall have it."

2

Political Career

Tilak founded the Marathi daily *Kesari* (Lion) in 1880. In just two years 'Kesari' attracted more readers than any language news papers in India. The editorials gave a vivid picture of the people's sufferings and of actual happenings. They called upon every Indian to fight for his right.

The language was so sharp as to create in the most cowardly reader the thirst for freedom. Tilak used to say to his colleagues: "You are not writing for the university students. Imagine you are talking to a villager. Be sure of your facts. Let your words be clear as day light." Tilak strongly criticized the government for its brutality in suppressing free expression, especially in face of protests against the division of Bengal in 1905, and for denigrating India's culture, its people and heritage. He demanded that the British immediately give Indians the right to self-government.

Tilak joined the Indian National Congress in the 1890s, but soon fell into opposition of its liberal-moderate attitude towards the fight for self-government. In 1891 Tilak opposed the Age of Consent bill introduced after the death of a child bride from sexual injuries. The act raised the marriageable age of a child bride from 10 to 12 which was already 16 in Britain since 1885. This was one of the first significant reforms introduced by the British since Indian rebellion of 1857. The Congress and other liberals wholeheartedly supported it but Tilak raised a battle-cry terming it as 'Interference in Hindu

Religion'. Since then he was seen as a hard-core Hindu nationalist. When in 1897, bubonic plague spread from Bombay to Pune the Government became jittery. The Assistant Collector of Pune, Mr. Rand, and his associates employed extremely severe and brutal methods to stop the spread of the disease by destroying even "clean homes." Even people who were not infected were carried away and in some cases, the carriers even looted property of the affected people.

When the authorities turned a blind eye to all these excesses, furious Tilak took up the people's cause by publishing inflammatory articles in his paper *Kesari*, quoting the Hindu scripture, the Bhagavad Gita, to say that no blame could be attached to anyone who killed an oppressor without any thought of reward. Following this, on 27 June, Rand and his assistant were killed. Tilak was charged with incitement to murder and sentenced to 18 months' imprisonment. When he emerged from prison, he had become a national hero and adopted a new slogan, "Swaraj (Self-Rule) is my birth right and I will have it."

Tilak opposed the moderate views of Gopal Krishna Gokhale, and was supported by fellow Indian nationalists Bipin Chandra Pal in Bengal and Lala Lajpat Rai in Punjab. They were referred to as the Lal-Bal-Pal triumvirate. In 1907, the annual session of the Congress Party was held at Surat (Gujarat). Trouble broke out between the moderate and the extremist factions of the party over the selection of the new president of the Congress and the party split into the *Garam Dal* ("Hot Faction," or extremists), led by Tilak, Pal and Lajpat Rai, and the *Naram Dal* ("Soft Faction," or moderates).

On 30 April 1908 two Bengali youths, Prafulla Chaki and Kudiram Bose, threw a bomb on a carriage at Muzzafurpur in order to kill a District Judge Douglass Kenford but erroneously killed some women travelling in it. While Chaki committed suicide when caught, Bose was tried and hanged. British papers screamed for vengeance and their shrill cries became even more insistent when Police raided and found a cache of arms at Calcutta. But Tilak in his paper Kesari defended the revolutionaries and called for immediate Swaraj or

Self-rule. The Government swiftly arrested him for sedition. He asked a young Muhammad Ali Jinnah to represent him. But the British judge convicted him and he was imprisoned from 1908 to 1914 in Mandalay, Burma.

Much has been said of his trial of 1908, it being the most historic trial. His last words on the verdict of the Jury were such: *"In spite of the verdict of the Jury, I maintain that I am innocent. There are higher powers that rule the destiny of men and nations and it may be the will of providence that the cause which I represent may prosper more by my suffering than my remaining free"*. These words now can be seen imprinted on the wall of Room. No. 46 at Bombay High Court.

Upon his release from Mandalay, Tilak re-united with his fellow nationalists and re-joined the Indian National Congress in 1916. He also helped found the All India Home Rule League in 1916-18 with Annie Besant and Muhammad Ali Jinnah. Tilak was impressed by the Russian Revolution, and expressed his admiration for Lenin. Tilak, who started his political life as a Maratha Protagonist, during his later part of life progressed into a prominent nationalist after his close association with Bengal nationalists following the partition of Bengal. When asked in Calcutta whether he envisioned a Maratha type of government for Free India, Tilak replied that the Maratha dominated Governments of 16th and 17th centuries were outmoded in 20th century and he wanted a genuine federal system for Free India where every religion and race were equal partners. Only such a form of Government would be able to safeguard India's freedom he added.

HIS DAYS IN THE POLITICAL ARENA

In 1897, bubonic plague scampered around Bombay and Pune claiming Government as one of it's victim.. The Assistant Collector of Pune, Mr. Rand, and his associates went on extreme and insane ways to efface the disease by demolishing even salubrious homes. Even people with no symptoms were forced into confinement and in some cases the carriers even plundered into the homes and got away with the loot. When the authorities became nonchalant towards these atrocities Tilak single handedly stood on the battle front and reaffirmed the fact that a pen is indeed mightier than a sword. He took a direct shot on it by publishing articles which incinerated the British fort. Few days later, on 27 June, Rand and his assistant met their makers. Charges of incitement to murder were pressed against him and was sentenced to 18 months imprisonment. His stay behind the iron bars only added to his iron will. After spending his days his captivity he came out and coined the slogan "Swaraj (Self-Rule) is my birth right and I will have it."

Tilak gave a tough resistance to the moderate views of Gopal Krishna Gokhale, and got his supporters in the form of Bipin Chandra Pal in Bengal and Lala Lajpat Rai in Punjab. They were looked upon as the Lal-Bal-Pal triumvirate. In 1907, the entire hell broke out in the annual session of the Congress Party and the differences between the moderate and the extremist factions of the party over the selection of the new president of the Congress became visible. Finally the party was fragmented into the Garam Dal ("Hot Faction," or extremists), led by Tilak, Bipin Chandra Pal and Lala Lajpat Rai and the Naram Dal ("Soft Faction," or moderates).

On 30th April 1908 driven by their intention to kill a District Judge Douglass Kenford, two Bengali youths, Prafulla Chaki and Khudiram Bose, threw a bomb on his carriage at Muzzafurpur but ended up killing some women travelling in it. While Chaki took away his own life when caught, Bose went through a trail and was sentenced to death. When every other English newspaper vilified the revolutionary only Kesari made pugnacious efforts to conserve the ideals of the great soul. The government didn't waste any time in arresting him for sedition. Later during 1908 to 1914, he spent his days in prison in Mandalay, Burma. The words uttered by him in his trial got etched on the walls of room No. 46 at Bombay High Court. Those were "In spite of the verdict of the Jury, I maintain that I am innocent. There are higher powers that rule the destiny of men and nations and it may be the will of providence that the cause which I represent may prosper more by my suffering than my remaining free"

On the onset of World War in August, Tilak established contacts with the King-Emperor in Britain and extended his hand of support. The Indian Councils Act, popularly known as Minto-Morley Reforms garnered his approval in May 1909 which had been passed by British parliament terming it as 'a marked increase of confidence between the Rulers and the Ruled'. He was keen to get at good terms with congress and disowned his demand for direct action and settled for agitations 'strictly by constitutional means.

LIFE AFTER PRISON

Tilak had mellowed after his release in June 1914. When World war I started in August, Tilak, cabled the King-Emperor in Britain of his support and turned his oratory to find new recruits for war efforts. He welcomed The Indian Councils Act, popularly known as Minto-Morley Reforms which had been passed by British parliament in May 1909 terming it as 'a marked increase of confidence between the Rulers and the Ruled'. Acts of violence actually retarded than hastened the pace of political reforms, he felt. He was eager for reconciliation with Congress and had abandoned his demand for direct action and settled for agitations 'strictly by constitutional means' - a line advocated his rival- Gopal Krishna Gokhale since beginning

All India Home Rule League

Later, Tilak re-united with his fellow nationalists and re-joined the Indian National Congress in 1916. He also helped found the All India Home Rule League in 1916-18 with Joseph Baptista, Annie Besant and Muhammad Ali Jinnah. After years of trying to reunite the moderate and radical factions, he gave up and focused on the Home Rule League, which sought self rule. Tilak travelled from village to village trying to conjure up support from farmers and locals to join the movement towards self rule. Tilak was impressed by the Russian Revolution, and expressed his admiration for Lenin. Tilak, who started his political life as a Maratha protagonist, during his later part of life progressed into a prominent nationalist after his close association with Indian nationalists following the partition of Bengal.

When asked in Calcutta whether he envisioned a Maratha type of government for Free India, Tilak replied that the Maratha dominated Governments of 17th and 18th centuries were outmoded in 20th century and he wanted a genuine federal system for Free India where every religion and race were equal partners. He added that only such a form of Government would be able to safe-guard India's freedom.

SOCIAL CONTRIBUTION

In 1894, Tilak transformed household worshipping of Ganesha into Sarvajanik Ganeshotsav. It is touted to be an effective demonstration of festival procession. But at the same time he supported caste system. He did not try any reform to break caste system. Gopal Ganesh Agarkar was the first editor of Kesari, a prominent Marathi weekly in his days which was started by Lokmanya Tilak in 1880-81. Gopal Ganesh Agarkar subsequently left Kesari out of ideological differences with Bal Gangadhar Tilak concerning the primacy of political reforms versus social reforms, and Gopal Ganesh Agarkar started his own periodical Sudharak.

PRESSURES OF LOYALISM DURING BRITISH RULE

Even as loyalist pressures cast a long shadow on political currents that were to influence the Indian elite of the late nineteenth century, rapidly deteriorating economic conditions also led to a heightened degree of radicalization amongst the most advanced sections of the new Indian intelligentsia. Ajit Singh in Punjab, Bal Gangadhar Tilak in Maharashtra, Chidambaram Pillay in Tamil Nadu and Bipin Chandra Pal in Bengal formed the nucleus of a new nationalist movement that tried valiantly, but mostly unsuccessfully to move the conservative leadership of the Indian National Congress in a more radical direction. Most charismatic amongst the new national leaders was Bal Gangadhar Tilak (b. 1856, d. 1920).

Portrayed as anti-Muslim by the Muslim-League, maligned by India's colonial rulers and British loyalists as an "extremist", and misrepresented as a sectarian Hindu revivalist by some historians, Tilak was in fact, one of the leading lights of the Indian freedom movement. Best remembered for his slogan *"Swaraj is my birth-*

right ", he was one of the first to call for complete freedom from British rule, and fought a long and sometimes lonely political struggle against the forces of "moderation" that held sway over the Indian National Congress in the early part of the last century.

After the defeat of 1858, one of the most significant challenges to British imperial authority in India had appeared in the form of Vasudeo Balvant Phadke's revolt of 1879, and amongst his many youthful followers and trainees in Pune was the young Tilak. Along with Chiplunkar, Agarkar and Namjoshi, Tilak initially concentrated on launching a nationalist weekly-the *Kesari* (1881), the publishing house-*Kitabkhana*, and developing Indian educational institutions such as the Deccan Education Society (1884).

Tilak and his friends saw the right kind of education as being a crucial element in the task of national regeneration, and in this respect appeared to be continuing in the tradition of Jyotirao Phule (1827-1890) and Gopalrao Deshmukh (1823-1892) who was more known by his pen-name 'Lokahitwadi'. Foremost amongst the social revolutionaries of nineteenth century Maharashtra, Phule and his wife Savitribai, had advocated a radical restructuring of Hindu society on the basis of equality of caste, gender and creed. Phule, (who belonged to the *Mali* caste) was unsparing in his criticism of Brahminical society that looked down upon the *shudra jatis,* prevented the *atishudra* (untouchable) *jatis* from attending school, and treated young widows (particularly Brahmin widows) as outcastes. One of the first to start a school for girls (1848), Phule went on to found the first school for the *atishudras* (1851), a home for young widows (1863), and also the first to open the family well to *atishudra* women (1868). Social reformers in Maharashtra also emerged from the upper castes, such as Gopalrao Deshmukh, who although a Chitpawan Brahmin was a sharp critic of Brahminical society, and worked primarily through reformist middle-class organizations such as the Prasthana Samaj and the Arya Samaj to fight against caste inequities.

But amongst Tilak's colleagues, not all were well-disposed towards Phule and Deshmukh (Lokahitwadi). Chiplunkar was particularly vitriolic in his criticism of Phule. Tilak, on the other hand, was not unsympathetic to the need for social reforms, and was opposed to evils like child-marriage, casteism and untouchability. Many years later, (at a conference in Bombay in 1918), he was to declare: *"If God were to tolerate untouchability, I would not recognize him as God at all"*. However, he was reluctant to give precedence to social reforms over political struggle, believing that social change ought to come gradually, through the growth of enlightened public opinion, rather than through the legislative authority of an alien government. He was convinced that no significant social progress was possible in a country that wasn't politically free. He was particularly critical of loyalist or moderate "reformers" who were unwilling to practice what they preached, yet frequently baited him as being against social reforms.

Neither a sectarian religious revivalist in the mold of Chiplunkar, nor willing to confine himself exclusively to the cause of radical social reforms like Agarkar, Tilak eventually parted ways with his colleagues in 1888. Working through the *Kesari,* (and later also the *Maratha*) he gradually developed a more advanced nationalist perspective based on the pillars of nationalist education, *Swaraj* (self-rule) *and Swadeshi* (self-reliance). One of the first to take the nationalist message to the Indian masses, he played a particularly important role in organizing western Maharashtra's peasant and artisan communities during the 1897 famine under the auspices of the Sarvajanik Sabha. By 1905, popular resistance movements had developed in both Bengal and Maharashtra, calling for the boycott of British goods and non-payment of land revenues and other taxes. Between 1905 and 1908 the national movement intensified, workers participated in strikes and work-stoppages, women and students joined the boycott movements-picketing at shops that sold imported goods, and an ever-growing mass of people began joining mass meetings and street processions.

Only too aware of the economic devastation that British rule had brought on the country, India's broad masses were responding eagerly to the nationalist message. But the nationalist movement was also becoming exceedingly divided between two poles representing radically different currents and tendencies. Whereas one side (even as it recognized the many negative aspects of alien rule) clung to the British umbilical chord, and attempted to restrict the national movement to a struggle for political reforms, the other side correctly saw British rule as an unmitigated disaster for the Indian people and called for the complete liberation from colonial rule.

Tilak eloquently and succinctly summarized the sentiments of the new and increasingly militant national movement. He spoke of British rule as having ruined trade, caused the collapse of industry, and destroyed the people's courage and abilities. Under the colonial regimen, Tilak asserted that the country was offered neither education, nor rights, nor respect for public opinion. Without prosperity and contentment, the Indian people suffered constantly from the three 'd's'-*i.e. daridra* (poverty), *dushkal* (famine) and *dravyashosha* (drain). And he saw only one remedy: for the Indian people to take political power without which Indian industry could not develop, without which the nation's youth couldn't be educated, and without which the country could win neither social reforms nor material welfare for it's people. Tilak saw colonial rule as being inimical to India's progress, and the contradictions between the British oppressors and the Indian people as being irreconcilable.

But "moderates" such as Gokhale (President of the Congress in 1905) while cognizant of how *"deplorable"* Britain's industrial domination of India was, and how the economic drain from India to Britain was *"bleeding India"*, were nevertheless all praise for the British educational system in India, ascribing to the British the virtues of introducing liberal "social reforms", governmental "peace and order" and such modern conveniences as the railways, post and telegraphs, and new industrial appliances. (That all these things benefited a miniscule Indian elite did not appear to bother such admirers of the empire, nor did it occur to them that this and much more could have just as easily been achieved under self-rule.)

Tilak and Gokhale were clearly seeing Indian reality from very different vantage points. From the point of view of the ordinary masses, British rule had already bankrupted the nation, left intolerable misery in it's wake, and offered no hope for the future. Tilak's assessment of the situation reflected bleak reality-as experienced not only by the oppressed and downtrodden Indian masses, but by an overwhelming majority of all Indians. But Gokhale's ambivalence and his more cautiously expressed (though clearly articulated) concerns reflected the position of those who had at least partially shared in the spoils of the empire, but saw with some trepidation how the growing poverty of the nation might unravel the British empire. Reluctant to make common cause with the masses, "moderates" such as Gokhale did everything in their power to restrain the growing national movement-even branding Tilak and his allies as "extremists".

The British took full advantage of this schism, and proceeded to bring the full weight of their administrative and military might in crushing the new national movement. Communal forces such as the Muslim League were also employed in the battle to extinguish radical tendencies. (See note below) The years 1905-1908 were thus extremely critical in shaping the direction of the Indian national movement. Increasingly, the Indian masses were looking to Tilak and his compatriots for direction. But, in direct opposition to the energizing of the Indian peasantry, and mass of workers and students across the country, the elite was reasserting it's loyalty to British rule.

In Punjab, the polarization was especially sharp. The boycott movement had struck deep roots within the peasantry, and made it difficult for British troops to find porters and other logistical help from the poor peasants. Roused by calls to protest the British land revenue policy, Sikh and Jat agricultural workers were becoming strongly politicized. In a rousing speech, Tilak's close associate in Punjab, Ajit Singh made a secular appeal to the masses of Punjab to rise against the British: *"Hindu brothers, Mohammedan brothers, Sepahi brothers-we are all one. The government is not even dust before us....What have you got to fear?....Our numbers are much greater. True they have guns, but we have fists...You are dying from the plague and other diseases, so better sacrifice yourselves to your motherland. Our strength lies in unity..."* (Excerpts from an April 21, 1907 speech in Rawalpindi)

On May 1, 1907, a spontaneous outburst of popular discontent shook the British administration in Rawalpindi when seething crowds, reinforced by striking workers marched through the streets-throwing mud and stones at passing Britishers, attacking government offices, cottages of Christian missionaries, British enterprises and commercial establishments. Although the uprising was effectively quelled by a large contingent of British troops who were close at hand, it shook the colonial administration enough to hastily evacuate families of colonial officials and military officers from Punjab, and extend term of the Commander-in-Chief of the British Army, Lord Kitchener. The colonial police and troops were also ruthless in crushing such uprisings in Lahore and Amritsar. Ajit Singh and Lala Lajpat Rai were summarily deported to Burma, without trial or right of appeal. Arrests and persecution of other patriots followed, and a state of emergency was declared in a number of Punjab districts. In 1908, uprisings on a similiar scale broke out in the South, in Trivandrum, Tirunelveli, and Tuticorin. In Trivandrum, police stations were attacked, prisoners liberated, and offices of the repressive colonial state were set on fire. When Chidambaram Pillay, another important Tilak ally was put on trial, he refused to disown his national goals, and was sentenced to life imprisonment.

Russian consular official Chirkin had been quite prophetic in his May 28, 1907 report when he wrote: *"The outburst in Punjab is by it's character more dangerous than the Bengal unrest..... This outburst has roused all India."* But equally powerful forces were working to stem and reverse the radical tide that had the potential of upturning colonial rule.

Bengal zamindars who had agitated against the partition of Bengal declared their loyalty to the Raj. The Maharajas not only offered armed personnel to help the British but some (such as the Maharaja of Jammu and Kashmir) themselves initiated repressive measures against those deemed "extremist".

The Congress who under the leadership of Dadabhai Naoroji had accepted the demands put forth by the Tilak group for Swaraj, Swadeshi and National Education in 1906, reneged on it's previous position, and at it's Surat session in 1907 decided to limit the struggle to a *"constitutional manner"*. *"Swaraj"* was reinterpreted to mean *"self-rule"* as a colony, and rather than fighting the colonial power, the Congress decided to cooperate with it in effecting *"reforms"*.

A motion to elect Tilak (who was unquestionably the most popular leader of the national-liberation movement) was turned down, as was a compromise motion to elect Lala Lajpat Rai. The triumph of the "moderate" wing was total and complete. Gokhale's "moderate nationalism" which was simply another face of loyalism succeeded to the utter exclusion of all the popular forces aligned with Tilak, and returned the Congress to a broadly loyalist track.

Tilak and his supporters were thus compelled to regroup outside the stifling confines of the Congress and continued a vigorous struggle against the British. But in July 1908, after having removed most of Tilak's serious compatriots from the national scene, Tilak himself was brought to trial. The English majority outvoted the Indian jurors to issue a guilty verdict, and Tilak was sentenced to six years of transportation. This evoked a mass protest wave which swept a number of Indian cities culminating in a massive strike of 100,000 workers and a city-wide 'hartal' (shutdown) in Bombay. Tilak's sentence had to be commuted to simple imprisonment, but it was sufficient to deal a severe blow to the Indian freedom movement.

By 1914, the Congress had so deteriorated that a majority of it's members failed to admonish the young Mohandas Karamchand Gandhi when he embarked on a campaign to seek volunteers for the British war efforts in World War I. The man who was to repeatedly chastise the Indian masses for being insufficiently "nonviolent", had in 1914, no compunctions in seeking sacrificial lambs for a war in which India's only interest should have been for the defeat of it's colonial master.

But Gandhi, who had been born the son of the Prime Minister of the princely state of Rajkot in Kathiawar, was simply following the lead of the Indian Maharajas, such as that of Bikaner-who needed little prodding in offering his troops for a war that essentially pitted Europe's older and stronger imperial powers against their emerging rivals.

Unsurprisingly, it was to Gokhale that the young Gandhi looked for inspiration, not Tilak. But others recognized his pre-eminent role in giving new direction and leadership to the Indian freedom movement.

Nehru pointed out that the *"real symbol of the new age was Bal Gangadhar Tilak"*, and recognized that *"the vast majority of politically-minded people in India favoured Tilak and his group"*. This was acknowledge as much by Sir Valentine Chirol, foreign editor of the *The Times,* who noted how Tilak's imprisonment deprived India of it's most able and determined leader, perhaps the only one capable of providing the Indian national movement (with it's different and often contradictory trends), the organization and unity that had been lacking thus far. N.C. Kelkar, a biographer and follower of Tilak echoed such sentiments.

Tilak and His Detractors-Charges of Communalism and Hindu Revivalism

An assessment of Tilak's role in the Freedom Movement has often been hampered by charges of "communalism" and "Hindu Revivalism". But a closer and more balanced inspection of Tilak's record in public life reveals a rather different picture. As early as 1888, Tilak had made a decisive break with his former cohort-Chiplunkar, unwilling to align with any narrow and sectarian agenda of chauvinist Hindu revivalism. This is not to say that Tilak was indifferent to Hindu traditions. Few leaders were. Many of the Muslim leaders were Maulanas, and Hindu leaders often had connections with the Arya Samaj or Brahmo Samaj. Tilak's interest in the Gita was neither exceptional, nor should it have brought any unduly unfavorable commentaries.

In fact, Tilak's interest in Hindu philosophy stemmed neither from conservatism nor from any tendency towards reactionary revivalism. Taken in the context of his vigorous contributions to the freedom movement, and the political clarity and directness of his message, it would be more appropriate to argue that his interest in his Hindu and Maratha heritage stemmed from the cultural vacuum that had been created by the alien and impersonal character of the British educational system. To find inspiration from ancient Indian texts, to find in the traditional Indian discourse, insights of contemporary value was for Tilak (and other leaders like him) not only something that contributed to developing self-awareness and self-esteem, it was as much an act of defiance towards the prevailing colonial-induced norms that ridiculed all things Indian, and valorized Western science and civilization to the exclusion of all else.

At a time when loyalist and "moderate" Indian politicians were enraptured by Western values and Western literature, discovering and connecting with Indian cultural traditions was not entirely without merit. In Tilak's case, it is especially important to note that he never counter-posed Indian tradition with Western scientific knowledge and technology. He was no xenophobe, and was all for India benefiting from the scientific and civilizational progress made in Europe. But unlike those that were utterly beholden to the colonial agenda, he saw no reason for educated Indians to eschew all interest in the Indian heritage either.

CLAIM OF THE SUPERIORITY OF HINDUISM

Tilak advocated the superiority of Hinduism over all other religions. During an address in Benaras in 1906 he said: "There is no other religion on the face of the earth except the Hindu religion wherein we find such a hopeful promise, a promise that God comes to us as many times as necessary. After Mahomed, no Prophet is promised, and Jesus Christ came once for ever. No religion holds such promise full of hope [....] A time will come when our religious thoughts and our rights will be vindicated"

According to Tilak, all the different sects of Hinduism are many branches of the Vedic religion. He claims that the term *sanatana dharma* ('eternal religion') shows that Hinduism is very old – as old as history of the human race itself. Vedic religion was the religion of the Aryans from a very early time.

Hindu religion as a whole is made up of different parts co-related to each other as many sons and daughters of one great religion. Tilak claims that all religions, except Hinduism, are partial truths. He says: "they [non-Hindu religions] are partial truth while our Hindu religion is based on the whole, the Sanatana truth". He adds: "Hindu religion is very comprehensive – as comprehensive as its literature itself; we have a wonderful literature. Wisdom, as is concentrated in the Gita and epitomised in about 700 verses, that wisdom, I am confident, cannot be defeated or overcome by any philosophy be it Western or any other".

In many of his speeches Tilak asked for greater co-ordination of all the sections of Hinduism under the banner of *Bharata Dharma Mahamandala* ('All India Religious Association'). He also emphasised the value of numbers. He said: "Numerical strength also is a great strength. Can the religion which counts its followers by crores die? Never, unless the crores of our fellow-followers are suddenly swept away our religion will not die. All that is required for our glorious triumph and success is that we should unite all the different sects on a common platform and let the stream of Hindu religion flow through one channel".

CLAIMS THAT HINDUISM IS THE MOST TOLERANT RELIGION

Tilak proudly maintained that Hinduism is the most tolerant religion in the world. According to him it tolerates all religions. He asks: "If there be any religion in the world which advocates toleration of other religious beliefs and instruct [sic] one to stick to one's own religion, it is the religion of the Hindus alone". He adds: "Shri Krishna does not say that the followers of other religions would be doomed to eternal hell. I challenge anybody to point out to me a similar text from the scriptures of other religions. It cannot be found in any other religion".

PROMOTION OF HINDU NATIONALISM

Koenraad Elst watches that Tilak was the first to associate Hindu imagery with the opportunity battle and he translated the Gita as far as political activism. It was amid the British decide that Hindu patriotism took birth. 'The father of Indian agitation' was in numerous regards one of the figures who sustained it. Tilak was a Hindu patriot to the center who made – as Walport says – no qualification amongst religion and legislative issues. He was against Muslim and hostile to Gandhi. As indicated by Tilak, religion is a component of nationality. He buttressed the cases of Hindu closed-mindedness through his grant. He said: "The normal figure Indian Society is the sentiment Hindutva (Hinduness)". The Hindu religion gives to the Indian culture a good and in addition social tie. Amid the Vedic times India was an independent nation and an incredible country joined by a typical culture. That solidarity vanished and it brought upon the country incredible debasement. In any case, it is the obligation of the pioneers of India to restore that union.

Tilak remained for the foundation of a Hindu rashtra in India. It is contended that Tilak had a section in the purported 'Nepal plot'. The thought probably was to persuade the King of Nepal to attack India, starting thus an uprising inside the nation in his support, since if the free King of the main autonomous Hindu Kingdom vanquished India there would be one sovereign Hindu country. Imitating of an incredible past is proverbial to any social renaissance. Tilak contended that truths that are being found by the West were known to the rishis of India. Present day science is bit by bit advocating and vindicating the old insight of India. He says: "Are not these basic devotions to the Vedas, the Gita and the Ramayana our basic legacy? In the event that we lay weight on it overlooking all the minor contrasts that exist between various organizations, then by the beauty of provision we should [...] have the capacity to combine all the diverse groups into a relentless Hindu country. This should be the aspiration of each Hindu".

The Gitarahasya is basically a work of patriot writing than of logic. Through it he made a mixing call to his comrades to activity so as to claim their bequest which is swaraj (self run the show). He contended that in that procedure it is honest to goodness to enjoy savagery, in impersonation of Arjuna and Shivaji. It is the rationale as opposed to the activity in-itself that matters. As it were, end legitimizes the methods.

INDOCTRINATION OF THE YOUNG THROUGH EDUCATION

Tilak was convinced that the salvation of his motherland lay in education of the people, which for him had to be English education. He was convinced that the mind arrives at a correct or incorrect decision according as it has been educated. In a speech delivered 1908 he spoke of the need for national education and religious education. He said: "We are not given such education as may inspire patriotic sentiments among us"; "We must have education on national lines, and for this there must be schools fully under the control of national leaders"; "Of the many things that we will do there, *religious education will first and foremost engage our attention*. Secular education only is not enough to build up character".

According to Tilak the want of religious education is one of the causes that have brought the Christian missionary influence all over the country. For the promotion of national and religious education, he first thought of establishing private schools on the model of the missionary institutions. Then he succeeded in founding the New English School without any help from the government, thereby establishing a model of education of the Indians for the Indians and by the Indians.

Tilak envisaged a Hindu university for Hindus. He said: "The idea of a Hindu University where our old religion will be taught along with modern science is a very good one and should have the support of all".

The success of Tilak's New English School paved way for its conversion into a public body called the Deccan Education Society under whose auspices the Ferguson College was founded (1885) for training educational missionaries for all of Maharashtra. Later, due to a conflict related to the management Tilak resigned.

BRITISH COLONIAL PERIOD—COLONIAL RULE (1858–AUGUST 1918)

After 1858, India turned out to be formally a British province as British crown took control of India from East India Company. The British crown put a Secretary of State for India in change of India. Indian Council who had just consultative forces helped him. India was isolated into three regulatory zones (Bengal, Madras and Bombay). Various managerial and legitimate changes were presented. In 1861 Indian Councils Act, High Courts Act and Penal code were passed. English kept on growing the railroads and transmitted system and in 1868 new Ambala – Delhi railroad line was begun. A blend of regulatory disappointments and characteristic elements brought about expansive number of starvations in India that murdered a large number of individuals:

1861 Famine in North West

1866 Famine in Bengal and Orissa – 1 million perished

1869 Intense famine in Rajasthan – 1.5 million perished

1874 Famine in Bihar

1876–78 Famine in Bombay, Madras and Mysore – 5 million perished.

During this time, India was forced to produce cash crop, which were to be sold by the British. India was also forced to accept British goods that destroyed cottage industries. Many peasants had to borrow money to pay the extremely high taxes imposed on them. 1st January 1877, Queen Victoria was proclaimed Empress of India at a *Durbar* (assembly of notables and princes), in Delhi. The Viceroy Lord Lytton represented the Sovereign, who incidentally never visited her Indian Empire. In 1878 Vernacular Press act was introduced in India that imposed severe limitations on the rights of the press. In the same year there was 'Rendition of Mysore' and Mysore was returned to its original Wodeyar rulers. In 1883 the Ilbert Bill Act was passed which allowed Indian magistrates to try Europeans. This angered the Europeans and the bill was withdrawn. Indians suffered from growing unemployment while most well paying jobs were reserved for the British. Racial discrimination against Indian's forced the Indian nationalists into organizing themselves for getting their demands accepted.

Hindu renaissance movement – During this period several great saints and religious leaders were responsible for revival of Hinduism in different parts of India. Ramkrishna Paramhansa (1836-1886), Swami Vivekananda (1863-1902) and Ishwar Chandra Vidyasagar (1820-1891) led the Hinduism renaissance in Bengal that later spread to other parts of India. Swami Dayananda Saraswati (1824-1883) formed Arya Samaj, which became a major religious movement in north India.

3

Tilak View on Vedic Myths

We have now examined most of the Vedic passages, which directly show that the Polar or the Circum-Polar characteristics, determined in the third chapter, were known by tradition to the Vedic bards. We started with the tradition about the night of the gods, or a day and a night of six months each, and found that it could be traced back to the Indo-Iranian, if not to the Indo-Germanic, period. A close examination of the dawn-hymns in the Rig-Veda next disclosed the fact that Ushas, or the deity presiding over the dawn, is often addressed in the plural number in the Vedic hymns, and that this could be accounted for only on the supposition that the Vedic dawns were a closely connected band of many dawns-a supposition, which was found to be fully borne out by express passages in the Vedic literature, stating, in unambiguous terms, that the Vedic dawns were 30 in number and that in ancient times a period of several days elapsed between the first appearance of light on the horizon and the rising of the sun.

We have also found that the dawn is expressly described in the Rig-Veda as moving round like a wheel, a characteristic, which is the true only in the case of the Polar dawn. These facts sufficiently prove the acquaintance of the Vedic bards with the physical phenomena, witnessible only in the Arctic regions. But to make the matter more certain, I have, in the last three chapters, quoted and discussed Vedic passages, which go to prove that the long Arctic nights and the corresponding long days of varying duration, as well as a year of ten months or five seasons, were equally known to the poets of the Rig-Veda. An examination of the ancient sacrificial system and especially of the annual *Sattras* and night-sacrifices, further showed that in old times yearly sacrificial sessions did not last for twelve months; as at present, but were completed in nine or ten months; and the hundred night-sacrifices were, at that time, really performed as their name indicates, during the darkness of the long night.

The legends of Dirghatamas and Aditi's sons, and the tradition about the sacrificial sessions of the Navagvas and the Dashagvas also pointed to the same conclusion. Our case does not therefore, depend on an isolated fact here and an isolated fact there. We have seen that the half-year long day and night, the long dawn with its revolving splendours, the long continuous night matched by the corresponding long day and associated with a succession of ordinary days and nights of varying lengths and the total annual period of sunshine of less than twelve months are the principal peculiar characteristics of the Polar or the Circum-Polar calendar; and when express passages are found in the Vedas, the oldest record of early Aryan thoughts and sentiments, showing that each and every one of these characteristics was known to the Vedic bards, who themselves lived in a region where the year was made up of three hundred and sixty or three hundred and sixty five days, one is irresistibly led to the conclusion that the poets of the Rig-Veda must have known these facts by tradition and that their ancestors must have lived in regions where such phenomena were possible.

It is not to be expected that the evidence on each and every one of these points will be equally conclusive, especially as we are dealing with facts which existed thousands of years ago. But if we bear in mind that the facts are astronomically connected in such a way that if one of them is firmly established all the others follow from it as a matter of course, the cumulative effect of the evidence discussed in the previous chapters cannot fail to be convincing. It is true that many of the passages, quoted in support of the Arctic theory, are interpreted, in the way I have done, for the first time; but

I have already pointed out that this is due to the fact that the real key to the interpretation of these passages was-discovered only during the last 30 or 40 years. Yaska and Sayana knew nothing definite about the circum-polar or the Arctic regions and when a Vedic passage was found not to yield a sense intelligible to them, they either contented themselves with barely explaining the verbal texture of the passage, or distorted it to suit their own ideas. Western scholars have corrected some of these mistakes, but as the possibility of an Arctic home in pre-glacial times was not admitted 30 or 40 years back, the most explicit references, whether in the Avesta or the Rig-Veda, to a primeval home in the extreme north, have been either altogether ignored, or, somehow or other explained away, even by Western scholars. Many of the passages cited by me fal! under this class; but I trust that if my interpretations are examined without any bias and in the, light of the latest scientific researches, they will be found to be far more natural and simple than those in vogue at present. In some cases no new interpretations were, however, necessary. The passages have been correctly interpreted; but in the absence of the true key to their meaning, their real import was either altogether missed, or but imperfectly understood. In such cases I have had to exhibit the passages in their true light or colours, giving in each case, my reasons for doing the same. This has sometimes rendered, it necessary to introduce certain topics not directly relevant to the question in hand; but on the whole, I think, it will be found that I have, as far as possible, tried to confine myself to the discussion of the direct evidence bearing on the points in issue and have examined it according to the strict method of historic or scientific investigation. I did not start with any preconceived notion in favour of the Arctic theory, nay, I, regarded it as highly improbable at first; but the accumulating evidence in its support eventually forced me to accept it, and in all probability, the evidence cited in the previous chapters, will, I think, produce the same impression on the reader's mind.

But the evidence, which I am now going to cite in support of the Arctic theory, is of a different character. If the ancestors of the Vedic bards ever lived near the North Pole the cosmical or the meteorological conditions of the place could not have failed to influence the mythology of these people; and if our theory is true, a careful examination of the Vedic myths ought to disclose facts which cannot be accounted for by any other theory. The probative value of such evidence will manifestly be inferior to that of the direct evidence previously cited, for myths and legends are variously explained by different scholars. Thus Yaska mentions three or four different schools of interpretation, each of which tries to explain the nature and character of the Vedic deities in a different way. One of these schools would have us believe that many of the deities were real historical personages, who were subsequently apotheosized for their supernatural virtues or exploits.

Other theologians divide the deities into *Karma devatas* or those that have been raised to the divine rank by their own deeds and *Ajana devatas* or those that were divine by birth while the Nairuktas (or the etymologists) maintain Vedic deities represent certain cosmical and physical phenomena such as the appearance of the dawn or the breaking up of the stormclouds by the lightening. The Adhyatmikas, on the other hand, try to explain certain Vedic passages in their own philosophical way; and there are others who endeavour to explain Vedic myths in other different ways. But this is not the place where the relative merits of these different schools can be discussed or examined.

I only wish to point out that those, who explain the Vedic myths on the supposition that they represent, directly or allegorically, ethical, historical, or philosophical facts are not likely to accept any inference based upon the theory which interprets the Vedic myths as referring to certain cosmical and physical phenomena. It was for this reason that I reserved the discussion of the mythological evidence for consideration in a separate chapter, after all the evidence directly bearing on the subject has been examined.

The evidence, which proves the existence of a long continuous dawn, or a long continuous day or night, is not affected by the different theories regarding the interpretation of the Vedic myths, and may therefore, be termed what the lawyers call direct; but in the case of mythological evidence only those who accept the Nairukta method of interpretation, will admit the validity of any inference based upon the consideration of these myths.

It is true that the Nairukta school of interpretation dates from ancient times, and that modern scholars have accepted the method almost without reserve, though they might differ from the ancient Nairuktas, like Yaska, in the details of the explanation suggested by them.

But still when a new theory is to be established, I thought it safer to separate the mythological from the direct evidence bearing upon the points at issue, even when the two lines of investigation seemed to converge towards the same point.

Now it has been recorded by Yaska that the Nairuktas explain most of the Vedic legends on the theory that they represent either the daily triumph of light over darkness, or the conquest of the storm-god over the dark clouds that imprison the fertilizing waters and the light of the sun. Thus when the Ashvins are said to have rescued a quail (*Vartika*) from the jaws of a wolf, Yaska interprets the legend to mean the release and bringing out of the dawn or light from the darkness of the night (Nir. V, 21). His explanation of the character of Vritra is another instance in point. Speaking of the nature of the demon, he thus refers (Nir. II, 16) to the opinions of the different schools, "Who was Vritra? 'A cloud,' say the Nairuktas; 'an Asura, son of Tvashtri,' say the Aitihasikas. The fall of rain arises from the mingling of the waters and of light. This is figuratively depicted as a conflict. The hymns and the Brahmans describe Vritra as a serpent. By the expansion of his body, he blocked up the streams. When he was destroyed the waters flowed forth."

The Storm and the Dawn theories thus formed the basis of the Nairukta school of interpretation, and though Western scholars have improved upon it, yet the credit of suggesting this method of interpretation will always rest with the ancient Nairuktas, who, as observed by Prof. Max Muller, had carefully thought out the true character of the Vedic gods several centuries before the Christian era. Thus the legend of Prajapati loving his own daughter is explained in the Aitareya Brahmana as referring to the sun running after the dawn or the heaven above (Ait. Br. III, 33); while Kumarila extends this theory to the case of Indra and Ahilya, which according to him represent the sun and the night. But though the Nairuktas fully accepted the theory, which explained the Vedic myths as representing cosmical and physical phenomena, yet as their knowledge of the physical world was very limited in those days, they were not able to explain every Vedic myth or legend by this method.

For example, out of 'the various legends about the Ashvins Yaska could explain only one by the Dawn theory, namely, that of the quail being rescued from the jaws of the wolf. This defect has now been partially removed by Western scholars, who, living in the more northern regions are familiar with the decay in the power of the sun during the cold season, or the eventual triumph of spring over winter or the restoration of the decayed powers of the sun in summer. This phenomena has, therefore, been used by them to explain the origin of certain Vedic myths, which have been left unexplained either by the Dawn or the Storm theory. Up to now, we have, thus, three theories for explaining the Vedic myths according to the Nairukta school of interpretation; and it is necessary to describe them briefly before we proceed to show how they fail to account for all the incidents in the myths and legends to which they are applied.

According to the Dawn theory, "the whole theogony and philosophy of the ancient world is centred in the Dawn, the mother of the bright gods, of the sun in his various aspects, of the morn, the day, the spring; herself the brilliant image and visage of immortality." Prof. Max Muller, in his *Lectures on the Science of Language*, further remarks that "the dawn, which to us is a merely beautiful sight, was to the early gazers and thinkers the problem of all the problems. It was the unknown land from whence rose every day those bright emblems of divine powers, which, left in the mind of man the first impression and intimation of another world, of power above, of order and wisdom. What we simply call the sunrise, brought before their eyes every day the riddle of all riddles, the riddle of existence.

The days of their life sprang from that dark abyss, which every morning seemed instinct with light and life." And again "a new life flashed up every morning before their eyes and the fresh breezes of the dawn reached them like greetings wafted across the golden threshold of the sky from the distant lands beyond the mountains, beyond the clouds, beyond the dawn, beyond the immortal sea which brought us hither." The dawn seemed to them to open golden gates for the sun to pass in triumph and while those gates were open their eyes and their minds strove in their childish way to pierce beyond the finite world. That silent aspect awakened in the human mind the conception of the Infinite, the Immortal, the Divine, and the names of dawn became naturally the names of higher powers. "This is manifestly more poetic than real. But the learned Professor explains many Vedic myths on the theory that they are all Dawn-stories in different garbs. Thus if Saranyu, who had twins from Vivasvat, ran off from him in the form of a mare, and he followed her in the form of a horse, it is nothing but a story of the Dawn disappearing at the approach of the sun and producing the pair of day and night. The legend of Surya's marriage with Soma, and of Vrishakapayi, whose oxen (the morning vapours) were swallowed by Indra, or of Aditi giving birth to the Adityas are again said to be the stories of the Dawn under different aspects. Sarama, crossing the waters to find out the cows stolen by Panis, is similarly the Dawn bringing with her the rays of the morning, and when Urvashi says that she is gone away and Pururavas calls himself Vasishtha or the brightest, it is the same Dawn flying away from the embrace of the rising sun. In short, the Dawn is supposed to have been everything to the ancient people, and a number of legends are explained in this way, until at last the monotonous character of these stories led the learned professor to ask to himself the question, "Is everything the Dawn? Is everything the Sun?" — a question, which he answers by informing us that so far as his researches were concerned they had led him again and again to the Dawn and the Sun as the chief burden of the myths of the Aryan race.

The dawn here referred to is the *daily* dawn as we see it in the tropical or the temperate zone, or, in other words, it is the *daily* conquest of light over darkness that is here represented as filling the minds of the ancient bards with such awe and fear as to give rise to a variety of myths. It may be easily perceived how this theory will be affected by the discovery that Ushas, or the goddess of the dawn in the Rig-Veda, does not represent the evanescent dawn of the tropics, but is really the long continuous dawn of the Polar or the Circum-Polar regions. If the Arctic theory is once established many of these mythological explanations will have to be entirely re-written. But the task cannot be undertaken in a work which is devoted solely to the examination of the evidence in support of that theory. The Storm theory was originally put forward by the Indian Nairuktas as a supplement to the Dawn theory, in order to account for myths to which the latter was obviously inapplicable. The chief legend explained on this theory is that of Indra and Vritra, and the explanation has been accepted almost without reserve by all Western scholars. The word Indra is said to be derived from the same root which yielded *indu*, that is, the rain drop; and Vritra is one, who covers or encompasses (*vri*, to cover) the waters of the rain-cloud.

The two names being thus explained, everything else was made to harmonize with the Storm theory by distorting the phrases, if the same could not be naturally interpreted in conformity therewith. Thus when Indra strikes *parvata* (*i.e.* a mountain) and delivers the rivers therefrom, the Nairuktas understood *parvata* to be a storm cloud and the rivers to be the streams of rain.

Indra's wielding the thunderbolt has been similarly interpreted to mean that he was the god of the thunderstorm, and thunderstorm implied rain as a matter of course. If the Maruts helped Indra in the battle, it was easily explained by the Storm theory because a thunderstorm or rain was always accompanied by stormy weather. But a more difficult point in the legend, which required explanation, was the hemming in or the captivating of the waters by Vritra or Ahi.

In the case of waters in the clouds it was easy to imagine that they were kept captive in the cloud by the demon of drought. But the Rig-Veda often speaks of *sindhus* or streams being released by the slaughter of Vritra; and if the streams or rivers really represented, as conceived by the advocates of this theory, the rivers of the Punjab, it was rather difficult to understand how they could be described as being hemmed in or kept captive by Vritra. But the ingenuity of Vedic scholars was quite equal to the occasion, and it was suggested that, as the rivers in India often entirely dried up in summer the god of the rainy, season, who called them back to life, could be rightly described as releasing them from the grasp of Vritra.

The Indian Nairuktas do not appear to have extended the theory any further. But in the hands of German mythologians the Storm theory became almost a rival to the Dawn theory; and stories, like that of Saranyu, have been explained by them as referring to the movements of dark stormclouds hovering in the sky. "Clouds, storms, rains, lightning and thunder," observes Prof. Kuhn, "were the spectacles that above all others impresses the imagination of the early Aryans and busied it most in finding terrestrial objects to compare with their ever-varying aspects, The beholders were at home on the earth, and the things on the earth were comparatively familiar to them; even the coming and going of the celestial luminaries might often be regarded by them with more composure, because of their regularity; but they could never surcease to feel the liveliest interest in those wonderful meteoric changes, so lawless and mysterious in their visitations, which wrought such immediate and palpable effects for good or ill upon the lives and fortunes of the beholders."

For this reason Prof. Kuhn thinks that these meteorological phenomena are the principal groundwork of all Indo-European mythologies and superstitions; and in accordance with this creed Prof. Roth explains Saranyu as the dark storm-cloud soaring in the space in the beginning of all things and takes Vivasvat as representing the light of heavens.

The third theory, like the first, is solar in origin, and attempts to explain certain Vedic myths on the supposition that they represent the triumph of spring over snow and winter. Yaska and other Indian Nairuktas lived in regions where the contrast between spring and winter was not so marked as in the countries still further north; and it was probably for this reason that the Vernal theory was not put forward by them to explain the Vedic myths. Prof. Max Muller has tried to explain most of the exploits of the Ashvins by this theory.† If the Ashvins restored Chyavana to youth, if they protected Atri from the heat and darkness, if they rescued Vandana from a pit where he was buried alive, or if they replaced the leg of Vishpala, which she had lost in battle, or restored Jijrashva his eye sight, it was simply the Sun-god restored to his former glory after the decay of his powers in winter. In short the 'birth of the vernal Sun, his fight against the army of winter, and his final victory at the beginning of the spring is, on this theory, the true key to the explanation of many myths where the Sungod is represented as dying, decaying or undergoing some other affliction. As contrasted with the Dawn theory the physical phenomena, here referred to, are annual. But both are solar theories, and as such may be contrasted with the Storm theory which is meteorological in origin.

Besides these three theories, the Dawn, the Storm and the Vernal, Mr. Narayana Aiyangar of Bangalore has recently attempted to explain a number of Vedic myths on the hypothesis that they refer to Orion and Aldebaran. This may be called the Astral theory as distinguished from others. But all these theories cannot be discussed in this place; nor is it necessary to do so, so far as our purpose is concerned. I wish only to show that in spite of the various theories started to explain the Vedic myths, a number of incidents in several important legends have yet remained unexplained; and mythologists have either ignored them altogether, or pushed-them out of the way as insignificant or immaterial. If everything could be explained by the Dawn or the Storm theory, we may indeed hesitate to accept a new theory for which there would then be very little scope; but when a number of facts, which have yet remained unexplained, are satisfactorily and appropriately accounted for only by the Arctic theory, we shall be perfectly justified in citing these legends as corroborative evidence in support of our new theory. It is from this point of view that I mean to examine some of the important Vedic myths in this and the following chapter, and shall now begin with the legend of Indra and Vritra, or of captive waters, which is generally believed to have been satisfactorily explained by the Storm theory.

The struggle between Indra and Vritra is represented in the Vedas as being four-fold in character. First, it is a struggle between Indra and Vritra, the latter of whom appears also under thee names of

Namuchi, Shushna, Shambara, Vala, Pipru, Kuyava and others. This is *Vritra-turya*, or the fight or struggle with Vritra. Secondly, it is a fight for the waters, which either in the form of *sindhus* (rivers) or as *apah* (simple floods), are often described as released or liberated by the slaughter of Vritra. This is *ap-turya* or the struggle for waters; and Indra is called *apsu-jit* or conquering in the waters, while Vritra is described as encompassing them (*apah pari-shayanam*). Thirdly, it is a struggle to regain the cows (*go-ishti*); and there are several passages in the Rig-Veda where the cows are said to have been released by India after having overthrown Vritra. Fourthly, it is a fight to regain the day-light or heaven called (*div-ishti*), or the striving for day; and in many places the sun and the dawn; are, said to be brought out by Indra after killing Vritra. The following extracts from Macdonell's *Vedic Mythology* give the requisite authorities from the Rig-Veda for this four-fold character of the struggle between Indra and Vritra.

Speaking of the terrible conflict, he thus sums up the principal incidents thereof as mentioned in the Rig-Veda: "Heaven and earth trembled with fear when India strikes Vritra with his bolt (I, 80, 11; II, 11, 9-10; VI, 17, 9), even Tvashtri who forged the bolt, trembles at Indra's anger (I, 80, 14). Indra shatters Vritra with bolt (I, 32, 5); and strikes his face with his pointed weapon (I, 52, 15). He smote Vritra, who encompassed the waters (VI, 20, 2), or the dragon that lay around (*pari-shayanam*) the waters (IV, 19, 2); he overcame the dragon lying on the waters (V, 30, 6). He slew the dragon hidden in the water and obstructing the waters and the sky (II, 11, 5), and smote Vritra, who enclosed the waters, like a tree, with the bolt (II, 14, 2). Thus The exploits of Indra are very pithily summed up in the *Nivids* or short Sutras or sentences used in offering oblations to the gods. These will be found collected in a separate chapter amongst the *Pari-shichtas* or supplements to the Rig-Veda Samhita text published in Bombay (Tatvavivechaka Press). According to Dr. Haug these *Nivids* are the originals of the Vedic *Suktas* or hymns. As regards the meaning of *Div-ichmi* see Oldenberg's Vedic Hymns (I, 45, 7), S. B. E. Series, Vol. XLVI. p. 44. conquering in the waters (*apsu-jit*) is his exclusive attribute (VIII, 36, 1)."

As regards the abode of Vritra, we have (§ 68, A): "Vritra has a hidden (*ninya*) abode, whence the waters, when released by Indra, escape, overflowing the demon (I, 32, 10). Vritra lies on the waters (I, 121, 11; II, 11, 9), or enveloped by the waters, at the bottom (*budhna*) of the *rajas* or aerial space (I, 52, 6). He is also described as lying on a summit (*sanu*), when Indra made the waters to flow (I, 80, 5). Vritra has fortresses, which Indra shatters when he slays him (X, 89, 7), and which are ninety-nine in number (VIII, 93, 2; VII, 19, 5). He is called *nadi-vrit*, or encompasser of rivers (I, 52, 2), and in one passage *parvata* or cloud is described as being within his belly (I, 54, 10)."

There are again passages (V, 32, 5 & 6) where India is said to have placed Shushna, who was anxious to fight, "in the darkness of the pit," and slaughtered him "in the darkness which was unrelieved by the rays of the sun," (*asurye tamasi*). In 1, 54, 10, darkness is said to have prevailed in Vritra's hollow side, and in II, 23, 18, Brihaspati, with Indra is said to have hurled down the ocean, which was "encompassed in darkness," and opened the stall of kine. Finally in I, 32, 10, Vritra's body is said to have sunk in "long darkness," being encompassed with waters. This shows that the waters of the ocean, which was encompassed by Vritra, were not lighted by the rays of the sun. In cther words, the ocean (*arnah*) which Vritra is said to have encompassed was different from the "bright ocean" (*shukram arnah*) which the sun is said to have ascended in V, 45, 10. Vritra's ocean (*arnava*) was enveloped in darkness (*tamasa parivritam*, II, 23, 18), while the ocean, which the sun ascended, was bright and shining (*shukram*). Indra is again described as going to a very distant (*paravat*) region to kill Vritra or Namuchi, (I, 53, 7; VIII, 12, 17; VIII, 45, 25). If we combine all these statements regarding the scene of the struggle between Indra and Vritra, we are led to the conclusion that the fight took place in a dark, distant and watery region. In VIII, 32, 26, India is said to have killed Arbuda with ice (*hima*); and in X, 62, 2, the Angirases, who were the assistants of Indra in his conquest of the cows, are said to have struck Vala at the end of the year (*parivatsare*). There is another statement in the Rig-Veda, which gives us the date of Indra's fight with Shambara, but we shall discuss it later on. It is stated above that the number of Vritra's forts destroyed by Indra is given as ninety-nine; but in other passages it is said to be ninety or one hundred (I, 130, 7; IV, 30, 20,). These fortresses or cities (*purah*) are described as made of stone or iron (IV, 30, 20; IV, 27, 1), and in some places they are said to be autumnal (*sharadih*, I, 130, 7; 131, 4; VI, 20, 10). The importance of these facts, in the interpretation of the legend, will be discussed later on.

We have seen that the release of cows and the bringing up of the dawn and the sun are the simultaneous effects of Indra's conquest of Vritra. The following extract from Macdonell's *Vedic Mythology* (p. 61) give the necessary authorities on the point: "With the liberation of waters is connected the winning of light, sun and dawn. Indra won light and the divine waters (III, 34, 8), the god is invoked to slay Vritra and win the light, (VIII, 89, 4). When Indra had slain the dragon Vritra with his metallic bolt releasing the waters for man, he placed the sun visibly in the heavens (I, 51, 4; 52, 8). Indra, the dragon-slayer, set in motion the flood of waters of the seat generated the sun and found the cows (II, 19, 3). He gained the sun and the waters after slaying the demon (III, 33, 8-9) When Indra slew the chief of the dragons and released the waters from the mountain, he generated the sung the sky and the dawn (I, 32, 4; VI, 30, 5). The cows are also mentioned along with the sun and the dawn, (I, 62, 5; II, 12, 7; VI, 17, 5), or with the sun alone (I, 7, 3; II, 19, 3; X, 138, 2), as being found, delivered or won by Indra."

Indra is described in other passages as having released the streams pent up by the dragon (II, 11, 2), and he is said to have won the cows and made the seven rivers flow (I, 32, 12; II, 12, 12). In II, 15, 6, the streams released by him have been described as flowing *upwards* (*udancham*). It may be further noticed that in all these passages the clouds are not referred to under their ordinary name *abhra*; but the words used are *parvata*, *giri*, *adri*, (which primarily mean a mountain), or *udhas* (udder), *utsa* (spring) *kabandha* (cask) or *kosha* (pail). All these words have been interpreted by the Nairuktas as meaning a cloud, and this interpretation has been accepted by Western scholars. The word *go*, which generally means cow, is also interpreted in some cases to mean the waters released by Indra. Thus when Indra is said to have released the cows, which were fast within the stone (VI, 43, 3), or when he is said to have moved the rock, which encompassed the cows, from its place (VI, 17, 5), it is understood that the reference is to a cloud-rock, which imprisons the rain-waters. Maruts are the usual companions of Indra in this, fight; but Vishnu, Agni, and Brihaspati are also spoken of as assisting him in the rescue of the cows from the grip of Vala. Brihaspati's conquest of Vala who had taken shelter in a rock, is thus taken to be a paraphrase of Indra's conquest over Vritra. In X, 62, 2 and 3, the Angirases are also described as driving out the cows, piercing Vala and causing the sun to mount the sky, — exploits, which are usually attributed to Indra. There are other versions of the same story to be found in Rig-Veda, but for the purpose in hand, we need not go beyond what has been stated above.

Now whosoever reads this description of Indra's fight with Vritra cannot fail to be struck with the fact that there are *four simultaneous effects* (Sakam, in VI, 30, 5), said to have been produced by the conquest of Indra over Vritra, namely, (1) the release of the cows, (2) the release of the waters, (3) the production of the dawn and (4) the production of the sun. Let us now see if the Storm theory satisfactorily explains the *simultaneous* production of these results from the destruction of Vritra. Vritra is a cloud, a storm-cloud, or a rain-cloud, hovering in the sky, and by smiting it with his thunder-bolt Indra may well be described as realizing the waters imprisoned therein. But where are the cows which are said to be released along with the waters? The Nairuktas interpret cows to mean waters; but in that cage, the release of the waters and the release of the cows cannot be regarded as two distinct effects.

The recovery of the dawn and the sun, along with the release of waters, is, however, still more difficult to explain by the Storm theory, or, we might even say, that it cannot be explained at all. Rain-clouds may temporarily obscure the sun, but the phenomenon is not one which occurs regularly, and it is not possible to speak of the production of the light of the sun as resulting from the breaking up of the clouds, which may only occasionally obscure the sun. The recovery of the dawn, as a prize of the conflict between Indra and Vritra simultaneously with the release of waters, is, similarly, quite inexplicable by the Storm theory. The rain-clouds usually move in the heavens, and though we may occasionally find them on the horizon, it is absurd to say that by striking the clouds Indra brought out the dawn. I know of no attempt made by any scholar to explain the four simultaneous effects of Indra's fight with Vritra by any other theory. The Storm-theory appears to have been suggested by the Nairuktas, because the release of waters was supposed to be the principal effect of the conquest, and waters were naturally understood to mean the waters, which we see every day. But in spite of the efforts of the Nairuktas and Western scholars, the simultaneous winning of light and waters still remains unexplained.

Macdonell (*Ved. Myth.* p. 61) referring to this difficulty observes, "There appears to be a confusion between the notion of the restoration of the sun after the darkness of the thunderstorm, and the recovery of the sun from the darkness of the night at dawn. The latter trait in the Indra myth is most probably only an extension of the former." If this means anything, it is only a confession of the inability of Vedic scholars to explain the four simultaneous effects of Indra's conquest over Vritra by the storm theory; and, strange to say, they seem to attribute their failure, not to their own ignorance or inability, but to the alleged confusion of ideas on the part of the Vedic bards.

These are not, however, the only points, in which the Stormtheory fails to explain the legend of Indra and Vritra. It has been pointed out above that Vritra was killed in distant regions, in which ghastly darkness reigned, and which abounded in waters; while in X, 73, 7, Indra by killing Namuchi, *alias* Vritra, is said to have cleared the gates of the Devayana path, evidently meaning that Vritra was killed at the gates of the path leading to the region of the gods.

Even in the Avesta, the fight between Apaosha and Tishtrya is said to have taken place in the sea of Vouru-Kasha, and Tishtrya is described as moving along the path made by Mazda after his fight with Apaosha. Vritra's abode is similarly described as "hidden" and "enveloped by water" at the bottom of *rajas* (I, 52, 6). None of these conditions is satisfied by making the storm-cloud, the scene of the battle between Indra and Vritra; for a cloud cannot be said to be the ocean of waters, nor can it be described as lying in a distant (*paravat*) region, or at the threshold of the Devayana or the path of the gods. In the Rig-Veda *paravat* is usually contrasted with *aravat*, and it means a distant region on the other side, as contrasted with the region on this or the nearer side. The Devayana is similarly contrasted with the Pitiyana, and means the northern celestial hemisphere. The clouds over the head of the observer cannot be said to be either in the distant region, or at the gate of the Devayana; nor can we speak of them as enveloped by sun-less darkness. It is, therefore, highly improbable that the rainclouds could have been the scene of battle between Indra and Vritra. It was the sea on the other side, the dark ocean as contrasted with the bright ocean (*shukram arnah*) which the sun mounts in the morning, where the battle was fought according to the passages referred to above; and the description is appropriate only in the case of the nether world, the celestial hemisphere that lies underneath, and not in the case of clouds moving in the sky above. I do not mean to say that Indra may not have been the god of rain or thunderstorm, but as *Vritrahan*, or the killer of Vritra, it is impossible to identify him with the god of rain, if the description of the fight found in the Vedic passages is not to be ignored or set aside.

The third objection to the current interpretation of the Vritra myth, is that it does not satisfactorily explain the passages, which give the time of Indra's fight with the demon. On the Storm theory, the fight must be placed in the rainy season or *Varsha*; but the forts of Vritra, which Indra is said to have destroyed and thus acquired the epithet *purabhid* or *purandara*, are described in the Rig-Veda as autumnal or *sharadih i.e.*, belonging or pertaining to *Sharad*, the season which follows *Varsha*. The discrepancy may be accounted for, by supposing that *Varsha* and *Sharad*, were once included under one season which was named not *Varsha* but *Sharad*. But the explanation is opposed to another passage in the Rig-Veda (X, 62, 2) which says that Vala was killed at the end of the year (*parivatsare*), unless we again suppose that the year commenced with *Sharad* in those days. Nor can we explain how Arbuda is said to be killed with *hima* (ice) by Indra. Again as previously stated, the dawn could not be considered as a prize of the conflict, nor could the fight be said to have been fought in darkness, if we choose the rainy season as the time for the battle of India with Vritra. It will thus be seen that the Storm theory does not satisfactorily explain the statements regarding the time of the struggle between Indra and Vritra.

The fourth objection against the Storm theory, as applied to the story of Vritra, is that many words like *paravat*, *giri*, or *adri*, which do not signify a cloud, either primarily on secondarily, have to be interpreted as referring figuratively to the rain-cloud. This sounds harsh in many a passage where Indra or Brihaspati is described as piercing a mountain or breaking open a *stone*-cave and liberating the waters or the cows confined therein. In the absence of any other theory, we had to interpret these passages by the Storm theory, as the Nairuktas have done, by assigning to any and every word, used to denote the prisonhouse of waters or the cows, the meaning of a rain-cloud moving in the sky. But though we could thus temporarily get over the difficulty, the fact, that we had to strain the words used, or to assign unnatural meanings to them, was always a drawback, which detracted from the value of our interpretation. It was probably for this reason that Prof. Oldenberg was led to suggest that Indra's piercing the mountain and liberating the waters therefrom should be understood to refer not to the rain-cloud, but to the actual striking of the mountains with the thunder-bolt and making the rivers flow forth from them. But, as observed by Max Muller, "the rivers do not gush out of rocks even when they have been struck by lighting"; and so Prof. Oldenberg's explanation, though it gets us out of one difficulty, lands us on another, which, to say the least, is equally puzzling.

If we, therefore, cannot suggest a better explanation, we might as well accept the device of the Nairuktas and interpret *parvata* or whatever other word or words may be found used to denote the place of the confinement of the waters, as meaning a cloud, and explain the legend of Vritra by the Storm theory as best as we can.

It will be found from the foregoing discussion regarding the Storm theory as applied to the legend of Indra and Vritra, that it explains neither the simultaneous effects of Indra's conquest over

Vritra, nor the statements regarding the seat of the battle between them, nor those regarding the time when it took place, nor again does it allow us to take the words, used in certain Vedic passages, in their natural sense; and yet we find that the theory has been accepted as the basis of the legend from the times of the Nairuktas up to the present. Why should it be so? — is a question, which would naturally occur to any one, who examines the subject. It is true that the Storm theory fully explains the release of waters as a result of the fight; but the release of waters is not the only consequence, which we have to account for. There are four simultaneous effects of the war, the release of the waters, the release of the cows, the recovery of the dawn and the production of the sun. The Storm theory explains the first two and the Dawn theory the last two of these; but the whole set of four is explained by neither, nor could the theories be so combined as to explain all the four effects, unless, like Prof. Macdonell, we suppose that the Vedic bards have confused the two entirely different ideas, *viz.*, the restoration of the sunlight after thunderstorm and the recovery of light from the darkness of night. Of the two theories, the Storm and the Dawn, the ancient Nairuktas, therefore, seem to have adopted that which adequately accounted for the release of the waters and which suited better with their notion of Indra as a thunder-god, on the principle that half a loaf is better than none, and have ignored the remaining incidents in the legend as inexplicable, unimportant, or immaterial.

The same theory has also been adopted by Western scholars, and it is the only theory in the field at present. But it is so manifestly inadequate that if a better theory could be found which will explain most of, if not all, the incidents in the legend, no one would hesitate to abandon the Storm theory in favour of the latter.

It is, in my opinion, a mistake to suppose that the struggle between Indra and Vritra *originally* represented the conflict between the thunder-god and the rain-cloud. It is really a struggle between the powers of light and darkness and we find traces of it in the Aitareya Brahmana (IV, 15.), where Indra alone of all gods is described as having under taken the task of driving out Asuras from the darkness of the night.

That Indra is the god of light is also evident from many other passages in the Rig-Veda, where, without any reference to the Vritra fight, Indra is said to have found the light (III, 34, 4; VIII, 15, 5; X, 43, 4) in the darkness (I, 100, 8; IV, 16, 4), or to have produced the dawn as well as the sun (II, 12, 7; 21, 4; III, 31, 15), or opened the darkness with the dawn and the sun (I, 62, 5). It was he, who made the sun to shine (VIII, 3, 6), and mount in the sky (I, 7, 1), or prepared a path for the sun (X, 111, 3), or found the sun in "the darkness in which he resided" (III, 39, 5). It is evident from these passages that Indra is the winner of light and the sun and this character of his was well understood by scholars, for Indra as *apavaryan*, or the recoverer (fr. *apa-vri*) of light, is compared by Max Muller with Apollon in the Greek mythology. But scholars have found it difficult to explain why this character of Indra should be mentioned in conjunction with other exploits, such as the conquest of Vritra and the liberation of the waters. In fact that is the real difficulty in the explanation of the legend either by the Storm or by the Dawn theory. Indra liberated the waters and brought about the dawn by killing Vritra, — is undoubtedly the burden of the whole story; but no explanation has yet been found by which the simultaneous recovery of light and waters could satisfactorily be accounted for. We have seen that by the Storm theory we can account for they release of waters, but not the recovery of the dawn; while if the legend is taken to represent a struggle between light and darkness, as implied by the Dawn theory, we can account for the recovery of the dawn and the sun, but not for the release of waters. Under these circumstances it is necessary to examine the nature and character of waters as described in the Vedas, before we accept or reject either or both of the above mentioned theories.

It has been noticed above that the passages, where waters are said to be released by Indra after killing Vritra do not refer expressly to the rain-cloud. The words *parvata*, *giri* and the like are used to denote the place where the waters were confined, and *apah* or *sindhus*, to denote the waters themselves. Now *apah*, or waters generally, are mentioned in a number of places in the Rig-Veda, and the word in many places denotes the celestial or aerial waters. Thus we are told that they follow the path of the gods, and are to be found beside the sun, who is with them (I, 23, 17). In VII, 49, 2, we have an express statement that there are waters, which are celestial (*divyah apah*), and also those that flow in earthly channels (*khanitrimah*, thus clearly distinguishing between terrestrial and celestial waters.

In the same verse they are said to have the sea or the ocean for the goal; and in VIII, 69, 12, the seven rivers are said to flow into the jaws of Varuna as into a surging abyss. Varuna again is described as the god, who, like Indra, makes the rivers flow (II, 28, 4); and we have seen that the sage Dirghatamas is said to have been borne on the waters wending to their goal (I, 158, 6). But it is needless to cite more authorities on this point, for scholars are agreed that both celestial and terrestrial waters are mentioned in the Rig-Veda.

The nature, the character, or the movements of celestial waters appear, however, to be very imperfectly understood; and this is the sole reason why scholars have not yet been able to connect the release of the waters with the recovery of the dawn in the Vritra legend. It seems to have been supposed that when the Rig-Veda speaks of the celestial waters (*divyah apah*) only the rain-waters are intended. But this is a mistake; for, in passages which speak of the creation of the world (X, 82, 6; 129, 3), the world is said to have once consisted of nothing but undifferentiated waters. In short, the Rig-Veda, like the Hebrew Testament, expressly states that the world was originally full of waters, and that there were the waters in the firmament above and waters below. The Shatapatha Brahmana (XI, 1, 6, 1), the Aitareya Upanishad (I, 1) and Manu (I, 9), all say that the world was created from watery vapours. There can, there fore, be no doubt that the idea of celestial waters was well-known to the ancestors of the Vedic bards in early days; and as the celestial waters were conceived to be the material out of which the universe was created, it is probable that the Vedic bards understood by that phrase what the modern scientist now understand by "ether" or "the nebulous mass of matter" that fills all-the space in the universe. We need not, however, go so far. It is enough for our purpose to know that the celestial waters (*divyah apah*), or the watery vapours (*purisham*), are mentioned in the Rig-Veda and that the Vedic bards considered the space or the region above, below and around them to be full of these celestial vapours which are said to be coeval with the world in X, 30, 10.

It is, however, alleged by Wallis in his *Cosmology of the Rig-Veda* (p. 115) that the Vedic bards were not acquainted with the regions below the earth, and that every thing, which is described in the Vedas as occurring in the atmosphere, including the movements of the sun during night and day, must, be placed in the regions of the sky, which were over the head of these bards. This view appears to be adopted by Macdonell in his *Vedic Mythology*; and if it be correct, we shall have to place all the waters in the upper heaven. But I do not think that Wallis has correctly interpreted the passages quoted by Prof. Zimmer in support of his theory that a *rajas* (region) exists below the earth; and we cannot, therefore accept Wallis' conclusions, which are evidently based upon prepossessions derived most probably from the Homeric controversy. Prof. Zimmer refers to three passages (VI, 9, 1; VII, 80, 1; V, 81, 4) to prove that a *rajas* beneath the earth was known to the Vedic people. The first of these passages is the wellknown verse regarding the bright and the dark day. It says, "the bright day and the dark day, both roll the two rajas by the well-known paths." Here the two *rajas* are evidently the upper and the lower celestial hemisphere; but Wallis asks us to compare this verse with I, 185, 1, where day and night are said "to revolve like two wheels," that is, to circle round from east to west, the one rising as the other goes down, and observes that "We are in no way obliged to consider that the progress of either is continued below the earth." I am unable to understand how we can draw such an inference from these passages.

In VI, 9, 1, quoted by Zimmer, two *rajas* or atmospheres are men tinned, and the bright and the dark day are said to roll along both these rajas or regions. But if we hold with Wallis that the progress of either begins in the east and stops in the west, without going below the earth, the whole movement becomes confined to one *rajas* or region and does not extend over the two. Zimmer's interpretation is, therefore, not only more probable, but the only one that explains the use of *rajasi* (in the dual), or the two regions, in the verse. The next passage (VII, 80, 1) is also misunderstood by Wallis. It describes the dawn as "unrolling the two regions (*rajasi*), which border on each other (*samante*), revealing all things. Now; the dawn always appears on the horizon and the two *rajas*, which it unrolls and which are said to border on each other, must meet on this horizon. They can therefore only represent the lower and the upper celestial sphere.

But Wallis would have us believe that both these *rajasi* are above the earth, and that narrowing down together towards east and west they meet on the horizon like two arched curves over one's head! The artificial character of this explanation is self-evident, and I see no reason why we should adopt it in preference to the simple and natural explanation of Zimmer, unless we start with a preconceived notion that references to the regions below the earth ought not to be and cannot be found in the Rig-Veda. The third passage pointed out by Zimmer is V, 81, 4, which says "O Savitri! Thou goest round (*pariyase*) the night, on both sides (*ubhayatah*). "Here Wallis proposes to translate *pariyase* by "encompassest;" but *pariyase* ordinarily means "goest round," and there is no reason why the idea of motion usually implied by it should be here abandoned. It will thus be seen that the conclusion of Wallis is based upon the distortion of passages which Zimmer interprets in a simpler and a more natural way: and that Zimmer's view is more in accordance with the natural meaning of these texts. But if an express passage be still needed to prove conclusively that the region below the earth was known to the Vedic bards, we refer to VII, 104, 11, where the bard prays for the destruction of his enemies and says, "Let him (enemy) go down *below* the *three* earths (*tisrah prithivih adhah*)."

Here the region below the three earths is expressly mentioned; and since the enemy is to be condemned to it, it must be a region of torment and pain like the Hades. In X, 152, 4, we read, "One who injures ms, let him be sent to the: nether darkness (*adharam tamah*)," and, comparing this with the last passage, it is evident that the region below the earth was conceived as dark. In III, 73, 21, we have, "Let him, who hates us, fall downwards (*adharah*)," and in 11, 12, 4, the brood of the Dasyu, whom India killed, is said to be "sent to the unknown nether world (*adharam guhakah*)." These passages directly show that region below the earth was not only known to the Vedic bards, but was conceived as filled with darkness, and made the scene of India's tight with Vritra. It may, however, be alleged that "below the three earths" may simply mean underneath the surface of the earth. But, in that case, it was not necessary to speak of all the *three* earths, and since we are told that the region is below *all the three* earths, it can refer only to the nether world. This is further proved by the passage which describes what is above the three earths.

The expression, corresponding to *tisrah prithivih adhah* or "the region below the three earths," will be *tisrah prithivih upari* or the region above the three earths," and as a matter of fact this expression is also found in the Rig-Veda. Thus in I, 34, 8, we are told that "the Ashvins, moving above the three earths (*tisrah prithivih upari*), protect the vault or the top of heaven (*divo nakam*) through days and nights"; and Ashvins are said to have come on their car from a distant region (*paravat*) in the preceding verse of the same hymn. The phrase *divo nakam* occurs several times in the Rig-Veda and means the top or the vault of the heaven. Thus in IV, 13, 5, the sun is said to guard (*pati*) the vault of the heaven (*divo nakam*); and as regards the threefold division of the earth it is mentioned in several places in the Rig-Veda (I, 102, 8; IV, 53, 5; VII, 87, 5), and also in the Avesta (Yt. XIII, 3; Yasna, XI, 7). In IV, 53, 5, this three-fold division is further extended to *antariksha*, *rajas*, *rochana* and *dyu* or heaven. This shows what we are to understand by "three earths." It is the one and the same earth, regarded as three-fold; and since the Ashvins are described as protecting the vault of heaven by moving "above the three earths," it is clear that in contrast with the vault above, a nether region, as far below the three earths as the heaven is above them, must have been conceived and denoted by the phrase "below the three earths," and that the latter expression did not merely mean an interterranean ground. When we meet with two such phrases as the heaven "above the three earths," and the region "below the three earths," in the Rig-Veda, phrases, which cannot be mistaken or misunderstood, the hypothesis that the Vedic bards were not acquainted with the nether world at once falls to the ground.

Mr. Wallis seems to think that since *rajas* is said to be divided three-fold, like the earth, and since the highest *rajas* is mentioned as the seat of waters, there is no scope in the Vedic division of *rajas* for a region beneath the earth; for the three rajas are exhausted by taking them as the rajas of the earth (*parthivam*), the rajas of the sky (*divo rajah*) and the highest (*paramam*) *rajas*, the seat of waters. But this objection is quite untenable, inasmuch as six different *rajas* are also mentioned in the Rig-Veda (I, 164, 6). We can, therefore, suppose that there were three *rajas* above the earth and three below it, and so meet the apparent difficulty pointed out by Wallis.

The three *rajas* can in some places be also interpreted to mean the earthly *rajas*, the one above the earth and the one below it, (X, 82, 4). In I, 35, 2, the Savitri is described as moving through the dark *rajas* (*krishnena rajasa*), and in the next verse we are told that he comes from the distant (*paravat*) region, which shows that the dark *rajas* and the *paravat* region are synonymous;, and that the sun ascends the sky after passing through the dark *rajas*. Again the use of the word "ascend" (*ud-yan* or *ud-acharat*, I, 163, 1; VII, 55, 7), to describe the rising of the sun in the morning from the ocean, shows,, by contrast, that the ocean which the sun is said to enter at the time of setting (X, 114, 4) is really an ocean underneath the earth. In I, 117, 5, the sun is described as sleeping in "the lap of *Nir-riti*," and "dwelling in darkness"; while in 1, 164, 32 and 33, the sun is said to have travelled in the interior of heaven and earth and finally gone into *Nir-riti*, or as Prof. Max Muller renders it, "the exodus in the west." Now, in X, 114, 2, there are three *Nir-ritis* mentioned, evidently corresponding to the three earths and three heavens; and in X, 161, 2, the lap of *Nir-riti* is identified with the region of death.

Pururavas is again said (X, 95, 14) to have gone to the distant region (*param paravatam*) and there made his bed on the lap of *Nir-riti*; while the Maruts are described as *mounting up* to the firmament from the bottomless *Nir-riti* in VII, 58, 1. All these passages taken together show that *Nir-riti*, or the land of dissolution and death, commenced in the west, that the sun lying in darkness travelled through the distant region (*paravat*) and eventually rose in the east from the lap of *Nir-riti*, and that the whole of this movement was placed not in the upper heaven, but on the other side of the vault through which the sun travelled before he entered into *Nir-riti*. In other words, the *Nir-riti*s extended below the earth from west to east; and since the region below the three earths is expressly mentioned in the Rig-Veda, the three *Nir-riti*s must be understood to mean the three regions belowthe earth corresponding to the threefold division of the earth or of the heaven above it. Zimmer is, therefore, correct in stating that the sun moved through the rajas below the earth during night and that the Vedic poets knew of this nether rajas.

There are other passages in the Rig-Veda which fully support the same view. Thus corresponding to the *rajasi*, or the two *rajas*, we have another expression in the dual, namely, *ubhau ardhau*, which literally denotes "the two halves," and when applied to heaven, "the two celestial hemispheres." The expression *ardhau* occurs in II, 27, 15, and the two halves are there asked to be propitious to the sacrificer. Wallis, however, interprets *ubhau ardhau* to mean "heaven and earth." But this is a mistake for there is a passage in the Rig-Veda where we have the phrases *pare ardhe* (in the farther half) and *upare ardhe* (in the nearer half) of heaven (*divah*), showing that the heaven alone (and not heaven and earth) was conceived as divided into two halves (I, 164, 12). A few verses later on (I, 164, 17), the cow with her calf (the dawn with the sun) is described as having appeared below the upper and above the lower realm, *i.e.*, between heaven and earth and a question is then asked "To what half (*ardham*) has she departed?" which again shows that the (*ardham*) here referred to is quite distinct from heaven and earth. In the Atharva Veda, X, 8, 7 and 13, the "two halves" are referred to, and the poet asks, "Prajapati with one half (*ardham*) engendered all creation; what sign is there to tell us of the other half?" Here the other half cannot mean the earth; and Griffith accordingly explains it as referring to the sun at night. Another expression used to denote the upper and the lower world is *samudrau* or the two oceans, (X, 136, 5). These two oceans are said to be one on this side (*avara*) and one on the other (*para*) side in VII, 6, 7; and a yonder ocean (*paravati samudre*) is mentioned in VIII, 12, 17. I have already quoted above the passages which speak of the bright *arnah* or ocean (V, 45, 10), and of *arnava* or an ocean pervaded with darkness (II, 23, 18). The two words *parastat* and *avastat* are also employed to convey the same idea. They denote a region on the nearer side and a region on the farther side. Thus in VIII, 8, 14, *paravat* region is contrasted with *ambara* or the heaven above, and in III, 55, 6, the sun is described as sleeping in the *paravat* region. We have seen above that Savitri is said to come up from the *paravat* region, and that he moves through the dark region before ascending the sky. The two words *paravat* and *arvavat* thus separately denote the same regions that are jointly denoted by the dual words *rajasi*, *ardhau* or *samudrau*; and when both the upper and the lower hemispheres were intended the word *ubhayatah* was employed.

Thus in III, 53, 5, we read, "O Maghavan! O brother Indra! go beyond (*para*) and come hither (*a*) you are wanted in both places, (*ubhayatra*)." The passages where Savitri is described as going round the night on both sides is already referred to above, With these passages before us, we cannot reasonably hold that the Vedic bards were ignorant of the lower celestial hemisphere, as supposed by Wallis, and some other scholars. Nor is the hypothesis a *priori* probable, for I have shown elsewhere that the Vedic bards knew enough of astronomy to calculate the movements of the sun and the moon tolerably correct for all practical purposes; and the people, who could do this, could not be supposed to be so ignorant as to believe that the sky was nailed down to the earth at the celestial horizon, and that when the sun was not seen during the night, he must be taken to have disappeared somewhere in the upper regions of the heaven. The passage from the Aitareya Brahmana (III, 44) which is quoted by Wallis, and which tells us that the sun, having reached the end of the day, turns round as it were, and makes night where there was day before and day on the other side, and *vice versa*, is very vague and does not prove that the sun was believed to return by night through a region, which is somewhere in the upper heaven. The words used in the original are *avastat* and *parastat*; and Dr. Haug correctly translates *parastat* by "what is on the other side."

Muir and others, however, interpret *parastat* to mean "upper," thus giving rise to the hypothesis that the sun returns during night by a passage through the upper region of the heaven. But in the face of the express passages in which regions below and above all the three earths are unmistakably mentioned, we cannot accept a hypothesis based upon a doubtful translation of a single word. It is a hypothesis that has its origin either in the preconceived notion regarding the primitive man, or in a desire to import into the Vedas the speculations of the Homeric cosmography. The knowledge of the Vedic bards regarding the nether world may not have been as exact as that of the modern astronomers, and we, therefore, meet with such questions in the Rig-Veda (I, 35, 7) as "Where is Surya now (after sunset) and which celestial region his rays now illumine?" But there is enough explicit evidence to prove that the Vedic people knew of the existence of a region below the earth, and if some of their notions about this underworld were not very distinct, that does not, in the least, affect the value of this evidence.

If we, therefore, dismiss from our mind the idea that the lower world was not known to the Vedic people, an assumption, which is quite gratuitous, the movements and character of the celestial waters become at once plain and intelligible. The ancient Aryans, like the old Hebrews, believed that the subtle matter, which filled the whole space in the universe, was nothing but watery vapours; and secondly that the movements of the sun, the moon and other heavenly bodies were caused by these vapours which kept on constantly circulating from the nether to the upper and from the upper to the lower celestial hemisphere. That is the real key to the explanation of many a Vedic myth; and unless we grasp it thoroughly, we cannot rightly understand some of the utterances of the Vedic poets. These waters were sometimes conceived as rivers or streams, moving in the heaven, and eventually falling into the mouth of Varuna or the nether ocean (VII, 49, 2; VIII, 69, 12). The nether world was, so to say, the seat or the home of these waters, called *yahvatih* or the eternal (IX, 113, 8) and they formed the kingdom of Varuna and Yama, as well as the hidden (*ninya*) abode of Vritra.

This movement of waters is very clearly expressed in the Parsi scriptures. In the Vendidad, XXI, 4-5 (15-23), the waters are described as follows, — "As the sea Vouru-Kasha is the gathering place of waters, rise up, go up the aerial way and go down on the earth; go down on the earth and go up the aerial way. Rise up and roll along! thou in whose rising and growing Ahura Mazda made the aerial way.

Up! rise up and roll along! thou swifthorsed sun, above Hara Berezaiti, and produce light for the world, and mayest thou rise up there, if thou art to abide in Garo-nmanem, along the path made by Mazda, along the way made by the gods, the watery way they opened." Here the aerial waters are said to start from their gathering place, the sea Vouru-Kasha, go up into heaven and come back again to the sea to be purified before starting on a second round.

Prof. Darmesteter in a note on this passage observes that "waters and light are believed to flow from the same spring and in the same bed", and quotes Bundahish, XX, 4, which says, "just as the light comes in through Alburz (Hara Berezaiti, the mountain by which the earth is surrounded) and goes out through Alburz, the water also comes out through Alburz and goes away through Alburz." Now waters are described in the Rig-Veda as following the path of the gods (VII, 47, 3), much in the same way as the waters in the Avesta are said to follow the path made by Mazda or the way made by the gods. Like the Avestic waters, the waters in the Rig-Veda have also the sea for their goal, and going by the aerial way eventually fall into the mouth of Varuna. But the Avesta supplies us with the key which establishes the connection of waters and light in unambiguous terms, for, as remarked by Prof. Darmesteter, it states clearly that both of them have the same source, and, in the passage quoted above, the swift-horsed sun is accordingly asked to go along the watery way in the skies above.

In the Aban Yasht (V, 3), the river Ardvi Sura Anahita is described as running powerfully from the height Hukairya down to the sea Vouru-Kasha, like the river Sarasvati, which is described in the Rig-Veda as tearing the peaks of mountains, and is invoked to descend from the great mountain in the sky to the sacrifice (V, 43, 11). Both are aerial rivers, but by coming down upon the earth they are said to fill up all the terrestrial streams.

The terrestrial waters, nay, all things of a liquid nature on the earth, *e.g.*, the plant-sap, the blood, *&c.*, were thus supposed to be produced from the aerial waters above by the agency of clouds and rain. The Parsi scriptures further tell us that between the earth and the region of infinite light (the *parame vyoman* of the Rig-Veda), there are three intermediate regions, the star region, which has the seeds of waters and plants, the moon region, and the sun region, the last being the highest (Yt. XII, 29-32). When the Rig-Veda, therefore, speaks of the highest *rajas* as being the seat of waters, it is not to be understood, as supposed by Wallis, that there are no nether waters, for it is the nether waters that come up from the lower world and moving in the uppermost region of the heaven produce terrestrial waters by giving rise to rain and clouds.

Thus Ardvi Sura Anahita is said to run through the starry region (cf. Yt. VII, 47), and has to be worshipped with sacrifice in order that her waters may not all run up into the region of the sun, thereby producing a drought on the surface of the earth (Yt. V, 85 and 90). In the Rig-Veda, the Sarasvati is similarly described as filling the earthly region and the wide atmospheric space (VI, 61, 11) and is besought to come swelling with streams, and along with the waters. But the most striking resemblance between Ardvi Sura Anahita and Sarasvati is that while the latter is described as Vritra-slayer or *Vritra-ghni* in Rig. VI, 61, 7, Ardvi Sura Anahita is described in the Aban Yasht (V, 33 and 34) as granting to Thraetaona, the heir of the valiant Athwya clan (Vedic Trita Aptya) who offered up a sacrifice to her, a boon that he would be able to overcome Azi Dahak, the three-mouthed; three-headed and six-eyed monster. This is virtually the same story which is found in the Rig-Veda X, 8, 8, where Trita Aptya, knowing his paternal weapons and urged by Indra, is said to have fought against and slew the three-headed son of Tvashtri and released the cows.

This clearly establishes the connection between waters, as represented by Ardvi Sura Anahita or Sarasvati, and the slaughter of Vritra. Many Vedic scholars have tried to identify Sarasvati with the river of that name in the Punjab; but as the latter is an insignificant stream, the identification has not been generally accepted. The above comparison now shows that the mighty Sarasvati, like Ardvi Sura Anahita, is an aerial stream, which rises up from the nether storehouse of 'waters, travels over the sky and again falls back into the lower ocean. A portion of these waters is brought down upon the earth in the form of rain by the sacrifices offered to the river, and along with it come the seeds of all the plants growing upon the surface of the earth.

Thus in the Vendidad, V, 19, (56), the tree of all the seeds is described as growing in the middle of the sea Vouru-Kasha, and the seeds are then said to be brought up by the aerial rivers and sent down by them to the earth by means of rain, an idea similar to that found in the Rig-Veda, I, 23, 20, where the sacrificer informs us that Soma has told him that all medicines (medicinal herbs) are contained in the waters. We have thus a complete account of the cosmic circulation of the aerial waters and the production of the terrestrial waters and plants there from. The nether world or the lower celestial hemisphere is the home of these waters, and it is expressly said to be bounded on all sides by a mountainous range like that of Hara Berezaiti. When the aerial waters are allowed to come up through this mountain, they travel over the upper hemisphere and again fall into the sea Vouru-Kasha, or the lower ocean, producing, during their course, rains which fertilize the earth and make the plants grow upon its surface. But instead of descending down in the form of rain, these aerial waters were, it was apprehended, apt to turn away into the region of the sun and deprive us of rain. It was, therefore, necessary to worship them with sacrifices and invoke their blessings.

It is impossible to grasp the real meaning of the Vritra legend, without first realizing the true nature and importance of the movements of the aerial waters as conceived by the ancestors of the Indo-Iranian people. As observed by Dramesteter, celestial waters and light were believed to flow from the same spring or source, and they both ran a parallel course. It was these aerial waters that made the heavenly bodies move in the sky, just as a boat or any other object is carried down by the current of a stream or river.

If the waters therefore, ceased to flow, the consequences were serious; for the sun, the moon, the stars, would then all cease to rise, and world would be plunged in darkness. We can now fully understand the magnitude of the mischief worked by Vritra by stopping the flow of these waters. In his hidden home, at the bottom of *rajas*, that is, in the lower hemisphere, he encompassed the waters in such a way as to stop their flow *upwards* through the mountain, and Indra's victory over Vritra meant that he released these waters from the clutches of Vritra and made them flow up again. When the waters were thus released, they naturally brought with them, the dawn, the sun and the cows, *i.e.* either days or the rays of the morning; and the victory was thus naturally described as four-fold in character. Now we can also understand the part played by *parvatas*, or mountains, in the legend.

It was the mountain Alburz, or Hara Berezaiti; and as Vritra, by stretching his body across, closed all the apertures in his mountainous range, through which the sun and the waters came up, Indra had to uncover or open these passages by killing Vritra. Thus the Bundahish (V, 5) mentions 180 apertures in the east and 180 in the west through Alburz; and the sun is said to come and go through them every day, and all the movements of the moon, the constellations and the planets are also said to be closely connected with these apertures.

The same idea is also expressed in the later Sanskrit literature when the sun is said to rise above the mountain in the east and set below the mountain in the west. The mountain on which Indra is said to have found Shambara (II, 12, 11), and the rock of Vala wherein the cows were said to have been imprisoned by the demon (IV, 3, 11; I, 71, 2) and which was burst open by Angirases, also represent the same mountainous range, which separated the upper from the lower celestial hemisphere, or the bright from the dark ocean. This explanation of the Vritra legend may sound strange to many scholars, but it should be borne in mind that the co-relation between the flow of water and the rising of the dawn and the sun, here described, is not speculative. If the Vedic works do not express it in unambiguous terms, the deficiency is fully made up by the Parsi scriptures.

Thus in Khorshed Yasht (VI, 2 and 3,) we are told that: "When the sun rises up, then the earth becomes clean, the running waters become clean.... Should the sun not rise up, then the Daevas would destroy all the things that are in the seven Karshvares." The passages in the Farvardin Yasht are still more explicit. This Yasht is devoted to the praise of the Fravashis, which correspond to the Pitis of the

Rig-Veda. These ancient fathers are often described, even in the Rig-Veda, as taking part, along with the gods, in the production of the cosmical phenomena. Thus the Pitis are said to have adorned the sky with stars, and placed darkness in the night and light in the day (X, 68, 11), or to have found the hidden light and generated the dawn (VII, 76, 4; X, 107, 1). The Fravashis in the Parsi scriptures are said to have achieved the same or similar exploits.

They are described (Yt. XIII, 53 and 54) as having "shown the beautiful paths to the waters, which had stood, before for a long time in the same place, without flowing"; and the waters are then said to have commenced to flow "along the path made by Mazda, along the way made by the gods, the watery way appointed to them." Immediately after (Yt. XIII, 57), the Fravashis are said to have similarly showed "the paths to the stars, the moon, the sun and the endless lights, that had stood before, for a long time, in the same place, without moving forward, through the oppression of the Daevas and the assaults of the Daevas." Here we have the co-relation between the flowing of waters and the moving forward of the sun distinctly enunciated. It was the Fravashis, who caused to move onwards the waters and the sun, both of which "had stood still for a long time in the same place." Prof. Darmesteter adds a note saying that it was "in winter" that this cessation of motion occurred, (Cf. Vend. V, 10-12; VIII, 4-10 cited and discussed (*infra*).

The Fravashis are further described (Yt. XIII, 78) as "destroying the malice of the fiend Angra Mainyu (the Avestic representative of Vritra), so that the waters did not stop flowing, nor did the plants stop growing." In Yasna LXV (Sp. LXIV), 6, the Fravashis, who had "borne the waters *up* stream from the nearest ones," are invoked to come to the worshipper; and a little further on the waters are asked to "rest still within their places while the Zaota (Sans. *Hota*) shall offer," evidently meaning that it is the sacrifice offered by the invoking priest that eventually secures the release or the flow of waters. There are other references to the flowing of waters (Yt. X, 61) in the Parsi scriptures, but those cited above are sufficient to prove our point. The main difficulty in the rational explanation of the Vritra legend was to connect the flow of waters with the rising of the dawn, and the passages from the Farvardin Yasht quoted above furnish us with a clue by which this connection can be satisfactorily established.

There are two passages in the Vendidad, which give us the period during which these aerial waters ceased to flow, and it is necessary to quote them here, inasmuch as they throw further light on the circulation of aerial waters. It has been stated above that according to Prof. Darmesteter these waters ceased to flow during winter, but the point is made perfectly clear in Fargards V and VIII of the Vendidad, where Ahura Mazda declares how the corpse of a person dying during winter is to be dealt with, until it is finally disposed of according to the usual rites at the end of the season.

Thus in Fargard V, 10 (34), Ahura Mazda is asked, "If the summer is passed and *the winter has come*, what shall the worshipper of Mazda do?" To which Ahura Mazda answers, "In every house, in every borough they shall raise three *Katas* for the dead, large enough not to strike the skull, or the feet or the hands of the man; ...and they shall let the lifeless body lie there for *two nights, three nights* or *a month long*, until the birds begin to fly, the plants to grow, the floods to flow, and the wind to dry up the waters from off the earth. And as soon as the birds begin to fly, and the plants to grow, and the floods to flow, and the wind to dry up the waters from off the earth, then the worshipper of Mazda shall lay down the dead (on the Dakhma), his eyes towards the sun." I have referred to this passage previously, but as the theory of the circulation of aerial waters was not then explained, the discussion of the passage had to be postponed. We now clearly see what is meant by the phrases like "floods to flow" and "plants to grow." They are the same phrases which are used in the Farvardin Yasht and are there connected with the shoving forward of the sun and the moon, that had stood still, or without moving, in the same place for a long time. In other words, the waters, as well as the sun, ceased to move during winter; and the worshipper of Mazda is ordered not to dispose of the corpse until the floods began to flow and the sun to move, be it for *two nights, three nights*, or a *month long*. The: Mazda-worshippers believed that the corpse was cleansed by its exposure to the sun, and dead bodies could not, therefore, be disposed of during night.

The passage from the Vendidad, above referred to, therefore, clearly indicates that the season of winter was once marked by long darkness extending over two nights, three nights, or a month; and that during the period, the floods ceased to flow and the plants to grow. It was during such a winter that the difficulty of disposing the corpse arose; and Ahura Mazda is asked what the faithful should do in such cases. The question has no meaning otherwise, for, if in the ancient home of the Mazdayasnians the sun shone every day during winter, as he does with us in the tropical regions, there would have been no difficulty in the disposal of the corpse by exposing it to the sun the next morning; and it would be absurd to ask the faithful to keep the uncleanly dead body in his house for two nights, three nights, or a month long, until the winter passed away.

The passage from Fargard V quoted, above makes no mention of darkness, though it can be easily inferred from the statement that the body is, at last, to be taken out and laid down on the Dakhma with its eyes towards the sun, evidently meaning that this ceremony was impossible to be performed during the time the dead body was, kept up in the house. But Fargard VIII, 4 (11), where the same subject is again taken up, mentions darkness distinctly. Thus Ahura Mazda is asked "If in the house of the worshipper of Mazda a dog or a man happens to die, and it is raining, or snowing, or blowing, or the darkness is coming on, when the flocks and the men lose their way, what shall the worshipper of Mazda do?" To this Ahura Mazda gives the same reply as in Fargard V.

The faithful is directed, VIII, 9 (21), to dig a grave in the house, and there "let the lifeless, body lie for two nights, three nights, or a months, long, until the birds begin to fly, the plants to grow, the floods to flow, and the wind to dry up the waters from off the earth." Here in the question asked to Ahura Mazda darkness is distinctly mentioned along with snowing and blowing; and in the Farvardin Yasht we have seen that the flowing of waters and the moving of the sun are described as taking place at the same time. The passage from Tir Yasht, where the appointed time for the appearance of Tishtrya after conquering Apaosha in the watery regions is described as one night, two nights, fifty, or one hundred nights has already been referred to in the last chapter. From all these passages taken together lit inevitably follows that it was during winter that the water ceased to flow, and the sun to move, and that the period of stagnation lasted from one night to a hundred nights. It was a period of long darkness, when the sun was not seen above the horizon; and if a man died during the period, his corpse had to be kept in the house until the waters again commenced to flow, and the sun appeared on the horizon along with them. I have pointed out previously how the Hindu belief that it is inauspicious to die in the Dakshinayana must be traced to this primeval practice of keeping the dead body undisposed of during the long Arctic night.

The word *Kata* which is used for "grave" in the Parsi scriptures occurs once in the Rig-Veda, I, 106, 6, where the sage Kutsa, lying in *Kata* is described as invoking the Vritra-slaying Indra for his protection; and I think that we have here, at least, an indirect reference to the practice of keeping dead bodies in a *Kata*, until Vritra was killed, and the waters and the sun made free to run their usual course. We are, however, concerned here only with the circulation of the celestial waters; and from the Avestic passages quoted above, it is clear that the aerial waters ceased to flow during winter for several days or rather nights, and that, since light sprang from the same source as waters, the sun also ceased to move during the period and stood still in the watery regions, until the Fravashis, who helped the gods in their struggle for waters or in their conflict with powers of darkness, made the waters and the sun move onwards to take their usual course in the upper celestial hemisphere. We can now understand why Indra is described as moving by his might the stream upwards (*udancha*) in II, 15, 6, and how the rivers are said to be set free to move on (*sartave*) by killing Vritra (I, 32, 12), or how in I, 80, 5, Indra is said to have made the lights of heaven shine forth without obstruction and set the waters (*apah*) free to flow (*sarmaya*). There are many other passages in the Rig-Veda where the flowing of waters and the appearance of the sun or the dawn are spoken of as taking place simultaneously, as may be seen from the quotations from Macdonell's *Vedic Mythology* given above, All these passages become intelligible only when interpreted on the theory of the cosmic circulation of aerial waters through the upper and the lower celestial hemispheres. But as the theory was little understood or studied in this connection, the Vedic scholars, ancient and modern, have hitherto failed to interpret the Vritra legend in a rational and intelligible way, especially the four simultaneous effects of the conquest of Indra over Vritra mentioned therein.

The cosmic circulation of aerial waters described above, is not peculiar to the Indo-Iranian mythology. Dr. Warren, in his *Paradise Found*, states that a similar circulation of aerial waters is mentioned in the works of Homer. Homer describes the sun as returning to the flowing of the ocean, or sinking into it, and again rising from it and mounting the sky. All rivers and every sea and all fountains and even deep wells are again said to arise from the deep flowing ocean which was believed to encircle the earth. Helios or the sun is further described as sailing from west to east in a golden boat or cup, evidently meaning that the underworld was supposed to be full of waters.

But Homeric scholars seem to have raised unnecessary, difficulties in the proper interpretation of these passages by assuming that Homer conceived the earth to be flat and that as the Hades was a region of complete darkness, the sun could not be said to go there even after his setting. Dr. Warren has, however, shown that the assumption is entirely groundless, and that Homer's earth was really a sphere and that the underworld was full of aerial waters. We have seen above, how some Vedic scholars have raised similar difficulties in the interpretation of the Vritra myth by supposing that the lower celestial hemisphere was unknown to the Vedic bards. This is probably a reflection of the Homeric controversy, but as pointed out by Dr. Warren, these baseless assumptions are clue mainly to a prejudice with which many scholars approach the question of the interpretation of ancient myths.

It is assumed that the early man could not possibly have known anything about the world, beyond what the rudest savages know at present; and plain and explicit statements are sometimes put aside, distorted, or ignored by scholars, who, had they not been blinded by prejudice, would certainly have interpreted them in a different way. It is impossible to do justice to the subject in this place, and I would refer to reader for further details to Dr. Warren's instructive work on the subject. Dr. Warren also states that Euripides, like Homer, held the view that there was one fountain of all the world's water, and that the same conception is expressed by Hesiod in his *Theogony*, where all rivers as sons, and all fountains and brooks as daughters, are traced back to Okeanos. Then we have the constant descending movement of all waters until they reach the world-surrounding Oceanriver at the equator, beyond which is the underworld, similar to the movements of aerial waters described in the Avesta. Aristotle in his Meteors, is said also to have mentioned "a river in the air constantly flowing betwixt the heaven and the earth and made by the ascending and the descending vapours."

It is again pointed by Grill that the ancient Germans had a similar world-river, and the descending Ukko's stream and the ascending Anima's stream in the Finnish mythology are similarly believed to be the traces of a like cosmic water-circulation. We read of a golden boat also in the Lettish mythology; and Prof. Max Muller, referring to it, says, "What the golden boat is that sinks into the sea and is mourned for by the daughter of the sky, however, doubtful it may be elsewhere, is not to be mistaken in the mythology of the Lets. It is the setting sun, which in the Veda has to be saved by the Ashvins; it is the golden beat in which Helios and Heracles sail from west to east. Sometimes it is the Sun-daughter herself that is drowned like Chyavana in the Veda, and as Chyavana and similar heroes had to be saved in the Veda by the Ashvins, the Lets also call upon the Godsons to row in a boat and save the Sun-daughter." In connection with this, it may be here observed that the Ashvins are described in the Rig-Veda as saving their proteges in boats (I, 116, 3; I, 182, 6), and that though Ashvins' boats are not described as golden, their chariot is said to be *hiranayayi* or golden in VIII, 5, 29; while the boats of Pushan, in which he crosses the aerial ocean (*samudra*) are actually said to be golden in VI, 58, 3. In I, 46, 7, the Ashvins are again spoken of as having both a chariot and a boat, as a sort of double equipment; and their chariot is said to be *samana yojana*, or traversing, without distinction, both the heaven and the watery regions in I, 30, 18. The word *samana* is meaningless unless there is some difficulty in traversing over one part of the celestial sphere as distinguished from the other.

The Vedic gods used these boats especially, in crossing the lower world, the home and seat of aerial waters; and when they appeared above the horizon, they are described as traversing the upper sphere by means of their chariots. But sometimes the waters are said to carry them even across the sky above, just as the chariot is described as going over the lower world. For instance in the legend of Dirghatamas discussed previously, he is said to be borne on waters for ten months and then growing old was about to die or reach the ocean, to which the waters were speeding. In other words, this means that the sun, who was borne on waters for ten months, was about to go into the lower watery regions as explained in the chapter VI. But to proceed with the subject in hand, the idea of the cosmic circulation of aerial waters, is not confined to the Indian, the Iranian or the Greek mythology. In the Egyptian mythology, Nut, the goddess of the sky, is sometimes "represented by a figure in which the band of stars is accompanied by a band of water"; and Sir Norman Lockyer tells us that "not only the Sun-gods, but the stars, were also supposed to travel in boats across the firmament from one horizon to the other."

The Jewish idea of the firmament in the midst of waters, the waters above being after wards separated from the waters below the firmament, is already referred to above. There is, therefore, nothing strange or surprising if we find in the Vedas and in the Avesta more or less clear references to the circulation of aerial waters through the upper and the lower celestial hemispheres of the universe. It is an idea which is found in the ancient mythology of every other nation, and nothing but false prejudice can deter us from interpreting the simultaneous movements or the liberation of waters and light, described in the Vedic hymns, on the theory of the cosmic circulation of aerial waters. But even after accepting the theory of the cosmic circulation of celestial waters and the simultaneous release of waters and dawn, it may be asked how the Arctic theory comes in, or is in any way required, to explain the Vritra legend. We may admit that the waters imprisoned by Vritra by shutting up the passages through the rocky walls that surround them, may be taken to mean the celestial waters in the world below the three earths; but still, the struggle between Indra and Vritra may, for aught we know, represent the daily fight between light and darkness, and it may be urged, that there is no necessity whatever, for bringing in the Arctic theory to explain the legend. A little reflection will, however, show that all the incidents in the legend cannot be explained on the theory of a daily struggle between light and darkness. In X, 62, 2, the Angirases, who are the assistants of Indra in his conquest of cows, are said to have defeated Vala at the end of the year (*parivatsare*). This shows that the struggle was annual and did not take place every day. Then we have the passage (VIII, 32, 26), where Arbuda, the watery demon, is said to have been killed by Indra with ice (*hima*), and not with a thunderbolt as usual. In addition to the fact that the struggle was an yearly one, we must, therefore, hold that the conflict took place during winter, the season of ice and snow; and this is corroborated by the statement in the Avesta, that it was during winter that the waters, and with them the sun, ceased to move onwards. Vritra's forts are again described as autumnal or *sharadih* showing that the fight must have commenced at the end of *sharad* (autumn) and continued during winter. We have further seen that there are a hundred nightsacrifices, and the duration of Tishtrya's fight with Apaosha is described as varying from one to a hundred nights in the Tir Yasht.

All these incidents can be explained only by the Arctic theory, or by the theory of the long autumnal night, and not on the hypothesis of a daily struggle between light and darkness. We have come to the conclusion that Indra's fight with Vritra must have commenced in *Sharad*, and lasted till the end of *Shishira* in the watery regions of the nether world. Fortunately for us this conclusion is remarkably borne out by an important passage preserved in the Rig-Veda, which gives us, what may be called, the very date of the commencement of Indra's conflict with Vritra, though the true bearing of the passage has yet remained unexplained owing to the absence of the real key to its meaning. In II, 12, 11, we read, "Indra found Shambara dwelling on the mountains (in) chatvarimshyam *sharadi*." Now *chatvarimshyam* is an ordinal numeral in the feminine gender and in the locative case, and similarly *sharadi* is the locative of *sharad* (autumn), which also is a word of feminine gender in Sanskrit. The phrase *chatvarimshyam sharadi* is, therefore, capable of two interpretations or constructions, though the words are simple in themselves. *Chatvarimshyam* literally means "in the fortieth," and *sharadi* "in autumn." If we now take *chatvarimshyam* (in the fortieth) as an adjective qualifying *sharadi* (in autumn), the meaning of the phrase would be "in the fortieth autumn"); while if the two words are taken separately the meaning would be "on the fortieth, in autumn."

Sayana and Western scholars have adopted the first construction, and understand the passage to mean, "Indra found Shambara dwelling on the mountains *in the fortieth autumn*, that is, in the fortieth year"; for the words indicating seasons, like *Vasant* (spring), *Sharad* (autumn), or *Hemanta* (winter), are understood to denote a year, especially when used with a numeral adjective meaning more than one. This construction is grammatically correct, for *chatvarimshyam* and *sharadi* being both in the feminine gender and in the locative case, the two words can be taken together, and understood to mean "in the fortieth autumn or year." But what are we to understand by the statement, that Shambara was found in the fortieth year by Indra? Are we to suppose that India was engaged in searching out the demon for 40 years, and it was only at the end of this long period that the enemy was, at last, found dwelling on the mountains? If so, Indra's conflict with Shambara cannot be daily or yearly, but must be supposed to have taken place only once in 40 years, an inference, which is directly opposed to the statement (X, 62, 2) that "Vala was killed at the end of the year (*parivatsare*)."

Some scholars try to get out of the difficulty by suggesting that the passage may be taken as referring to a famine or drought that occurred after 40 years, or that it may represent a forty years' war between the Aryans protected by Indra, and Shambara, the chief of the aboriginal races dwelling on the mountains! But both these explanations are too far-fetched and imaginary to deserve any serious attention or refutation. The story of Shambara is mentioned in a number of places in the Rig-Veda, and everywhere it represents

Indra's conflict with Vritra. It is, therefore, preposterous to hold that a forty years' war with the aborigines is referred to in this single passage, especially when the passage is capable of being interpreted differently without straining the words used. It is the most ordinary Sanskrit idiom to use the locative case in mentioning the month, the day, the season or the year, when a particular incident is said to have taken place. Thus, even now, we say, "*Karttike, shukla-pakshe, trayodashyam*," meaning "in the month of Karttika, in the bright half, on the thirteenth (*tithi* or day)."

The feminine ordinal numerals, like *chaturthi*, *ekadashi*, *trayodashi*, are always used, without any noun, to denote the *tithi* or the day of the month, or the fortnight, as the case may be. Thus in the Taittiriya Brahmana (I, 1, 9, 10), we have the expression "*yadi samvatsare na adadhyat dvadashyam purastat adadhyat*," meaning that, "if the sacrificial fire is not consecrated at the end of the year (*samvatsare*), it should be consecrated on the twelfth (*dvadashyam*) afterwards." Here *dvadashyam* is a feminine ordinal in the locative case used by itself, and means "on the twelfth *tithi* or day" after the end of the year mentioned in the preceding sentence.

Chatvarimshyam, in the Vedic passage under discussion, may be similarly taken to denote the *fortieth tithi* or day, and *sharadi* the season at the time, the two words being taken as independent locatives. The passage would then mean "Indra found Shambara dwelling on the mountains on the *fortieth* (scil. *tithi*) in autumn."

Now *Sharad* is the fourth season of the year, and the fortieth day of *Sharad* would mean seven months and ten days, or 220 days, after the first day of *Vasanta* or the spring, which commenced the year in old times. In short, the passage means that Indra's fight with Shambera, or the annual conflict between light and darkness, commenced on the tenth day of the eighth month of the year, or on the 10th of October, if we take the year to have then commenced with March, the first month in the old Roman calendar. In I, 165, 6, Vishnu, like a rounded wheel, is said to have set in swift motion his ninety racing steeds together with the four, and the reference is evidently to a year of four seasons of ninety days each. If we accept this division, each season would be of three months' duration, and

Sharad being the third (cf, X, 90, 6), the fortieth day of *Sharad* would still mean the 10th day of the eighth month of the year. The passage thus gives the very date of Indra's annual fight with Vritra; and if it had been correctly understood, much useless speculation about the nature of Vritra's legend would have been avoided. We have seen previously that the seven Adityas, or monthly Sun-gods, the sons of Aditi, were presented by her to the gods in a former *yuga*, and that she cast away the eighth, Martanda, because he was born in an undeveloped state. In other words, the Sun-god of the eighth month is here said to have died soon after he was born, evidently meaning, that the Sun went below the horizon in the beginning of the eighth month; and by fixing the date of the commencement of Indra's fight with Vritra as the fortieth day in *Sharad*, or the 10th day of the eighth month, we arrive at the same conclusion. The legend of Aditi and the date of the commencement of Indra's fight with Shambara, as given in II, 12, 11, thus corroborate each other in a remarkable way; and as the current interpretation of the passage does not yield any intelligible sense, there is no course left for us but to accept the only other possible interpretation.

According to this interpretation *Sharad* becomes the last season of sunshine, and it may be here remarked that the etymological meaning of the word further supports the same view. For *Sharad* is derived from *shri*, to wither or waste away (Unadi 127), and the word thus primarily signifies the "season of decay or withering"; and the decay here referred to is evidently the-decay of the power of the sun, and not the withering of grass, as suggested by Sayana in his commentary on III, 32, 9. Thus we find in the Taittiriya Samhita, II, 1, 2, 5, that "There are three lusters or powers of the sun; one in *Vasanta*, that is, in the morning; one in *Grishma* or the midday; and one in *Sharad* or the evening." We cannot suppose that the words, morning, midday and evening, are here used in their primary sense.

The three stages of the day represented by them are predicated of the yearly sun, and *Sharad* is said to be the evening, *i.e.*, the time of decline in his yearly course. It follows, therefore, that after *Sharad* there was no period of sunshine in ancient times; and a Vedic passage, quoted by Shabara in his commentary on Jaimini Sutras VI, 7, 40, says, "The sun is all the seasons; when it is morning (*uditi*), it is *Vasanta*: when the milking time (*sangava*) it is *Grishma*; when midday (*madhyan-dina*), it is *Varsha*; when evening (*aparahna*), it is *Sharad*; when it sets (*astam eti*), it is the dual season of *Hemanta* and *Shishira*."

If this passage has any meaning, it shows that the powers of the sun declined in *Sharad*, and the end of *Sharad* (autumn) therefore, represented his annual succumbing to the powers of the darkness; or, in short, to dual season of *Hemanta* and *Shishira* represented the long night when the sun went below the horizon. It may also be mentioned that the word *himya* (*lit.* wintry) is used in the Rig-Veda for night (I, 34, 1), implying but it clearly states that the last two seasons formed the night of the yearly sun that the wintry season was the season of special darkness. But it may be urged that we have no authority for holding that, in ancient days, time was reckoned simply by seasons and days; and *chatvarimshyam sharadi* cannot, therefore, be interpreted to mean "On the 40th (day) in *Sharad*." The objection is not, however, wellfounded; for in ancient inscriptions we find many instances where dates of events are recorded only by reference to seasons. Thus in the book on the *Inscriptions from the Cave-Temples of Western India*, by Dr. Burgess and Pandit Bhagwanlal Indraji, published by the Government of Bombay in 1881, the date of inscription No. 14 is given as follows: — "Of king (*rano*) Vasithiputa, the illustrious lord (*sami-siri*) [Pulumayi] in the year seventh (7), of *Grishma* the fifth (5) fortnight, and first (1) day." Upon this Dr. Burgess remarks that "the mention of the 5th fortnight of *Grishma* shows that the year was not divided into six seasons (*ritu*) but into three, namely, *Grishma*, *Varsha* and *Hemanta*." But what is important for our purpose in this inscription is the method of giving the date by seasons, fortnights and days, without any reference to the month.

This inscription is followed in the same book by others, one of which (No. 20) is thus dated: "In the twenty-fourth year (24) of the king Vasithiputa, the illustrious Pulumayi, in the third (3) fortnight of the winter (*Hemanta*) months, on the second (2) day"; and another is said to be inscribed "On the tenth day, in the sixth fortnight of

Grishma, in the eighth year of king Madhariputta, the lord Sirisena." Dr. Bhandarkar, in his *Early History of the Deecan*, has ascertained that Madhariputta reigned in the Maharashtra from about A.D. 190 to 197, and Pulumayi was on the throne of the Maharashtra about 60 years earlier, that is, from A.D. 130 to 154. All the inscriptions noted above, therefore, belong to the 2nd century of the Christian era, that is, a long time before the date of Arya Bhatta or Varahamihira, whose works seem so have established, if not introduced, the present system of measuring time by seasons, months, fortnights and days. It is, therefore, clear that eighteen hundred years ago, dates or events were recorded and ascertained by mentioning only the season, the fortnight and the day of the fortnight, without any reference to the month of the year; and we might very well suppose that several centuries before this period these dates were given by a still more simple method, namely, by mentioning only the season and the day of that season. And, as a matter of fact, we do find this method of measuring time, *viz.*, by seasons and days, adopted in the Avesta to mark the particular days of the year.

Thus in the Afrigan Gahanbar (I, 7-12), as written in some manuscripts mentioned by Westergaard in his notes ort the Afrigan, there is a statement of the different rewards which a Mazdayasnian receives in the next life for what he gives as present in this to the Ratu (religious head); and we have therein such expressions as "On the 45th (day) of Maidhyo-Zaremya, *i.e.*, on (the day) Dae of (the month) Ardibehest;" or "On the 60th (day) of Maidhyoshma, *i.e.*, on (the day) Dae of (the month) Tir;" and so on. Here each date is given in two different ways: *first* by mentioning the Gahanbar or the season (the year being divided into six Gahanbars), and the day of that season; and *secondly*, by mentioning the month and the day of that month. Strictly speaking there is no necessity to adopt this double method of marking the days of the year, for either of them is enough to accurately define the day required. It is, therefore, highly probable, as remarked by Mr. Ervad Jamshedji Dadabhai Nadershah, that the method of counting by seasons and days is the older of the two, and the phrases containing the names of the months and days are later interpolations, made at a time when the older method was superseded by the latter. But even supposing that the double phrases were used originally, we can, so far as our present purpose is concerned, safely infer from these passages that the method of marking the days of the year by mentioning the season and the day thereof was in vogue at the time when the Afrigan was written: and if the method is so old, it fully warrants us in interpreting *chatvarimshyam sharadi* to mean "On the 40th (day) in *Sharad* (autumn)."

There can be little doubt that the Vedic bards have recorded in this passage the exact date of the commencement of Indra's fight with Shambara, but in the absence of the true key to its meaning the passage has been so long unfortunately misunderstood and misinterpreted both by Eastern and Western scholars. The grammatical possibility of connecting *chatvarimshyam*, as an adjective, with *sharadi* helped on this misconception; and though Vedic scholars were unable to explain why Shambara, according to their interpretation, should be described as having been found in the 40th year, yet they seemed to have accepted the interpretation, because no other meaning appeared possible to them.

The alternative construction proposed by me above is very simple. Instead-of taking *chatvarimshyam* as an adjective qualifying *sharadi* I take the two words as independent locatives, but the change in the meaning caused thereby is very striking and important and so long as the Arctic: theory was unknown, the attention of scholars was not likely to be drawn to this alternative construction. But now we can very well understand why Indra is said to have found Shambara on the 40th (day) of *Sharad* and why the forts, which gave shelter to the demon, are described as *sharadih*, as well as why Arbuda or the watery demon is said to be killed by ice (*hima*). I have stated before that the forts (*purah*) of Shambara must be understood to mean "days," and the adjective *sharadih* only serves to strengthen the same view. The disappearance of the sun below the horizon in the beginning of the 8th month in autumn, followed by a long twilight, a continuous dark night of about 100 days, and a long dawn of 30 days in the Arctic regions, is the basis of the legend, and every incident therein can be naturally and intelligibly explained only on this theory.

There is one more incident in the Vritra legend which requires to be considered before we close its examination. We have seen that water and light are described as having been simultaneously liberated by Indra after slaughtering Vritra. These waters are sometimes spoken of as streams or rivers (II, 15, 3; II, 2), which flow *upwards* or *udancha* (II, 15, 6) and are said to be *seven* in number (I, 32, 12; II, 12, 12). The theory of the cosmic circulation of aerial waters explains why these waters are described as flowing *upwards* simultaneously with the dawn, for as the sun was believed to be carried in the sky by aerial currents, the light of the sun appeared above the horizon when the aerial rivers began to flow up from the nether world where they had been blocked before by Vritra. The waters or the rivers were, therefore, aptly described as flowing upwards and bringing the light of the sun with them. But we have still to answer the question why the rivers or waters are described as *seven* in number, and it is alleged that the Storm theory supplies us with a satisfactory reply to this question. Thus it has been suggested by Western scholars that the seven rivers, here referred to, are the seven rivers of the Panjaub which are flooded during the rainy season by waters released by Indra from the clutches of the demon who confines them in the stormcloud.

The rivers of Punjaub may therefore, it is urged be well described as being set free to flow (*sartave*) by Indra himself, and in support of this explanation we are referred to the Rig-Veda X, 75, and to the phrase *hapta hindu* occurring in Fargard I of the Vendidad, where it is said to denote the Punjaub or India. But the hypothesis, howsoever tempting it may seem at the first sight, is quite inadequate to explain the seven-fold division of waters in a satisfactory way. It has been pointed out above that the simultaneous release of waters and light can be accounted for only on the theory of the cosmic circulation of aerial waters; and if this is correct, we cannot identify the seven rivers, set free to flow *upwards* (*udancha*) by Indra, with any terrestrial rivers whether in the Panjaub or elsewhere. The Panjaub is, again, as its name indicates, a land of *five* and not of seven rivers; and it is so described in the Vajasaneyi Samhita. The term *panchanada* is, therefore, more appropriate in the case of the Panjaub, than *sapta sindhavah* or the *Hapta-hindu* of the Avesta. But we might get over the difficulty by supposing that Kubha and Sarasvati, or any other two tributaries of the Indus were included in the, group by the Vedic bards, when they spoke of seven rivers. In the Rig-Veda (X, 75), about fifteen different rivers are mentioned, including the Ganga, the Yamuna, the Kubha, the Krumu, the Gomati, the Rasa, and the five rivers of the Panjaub; but nowhere do we find what specific rivers were included in the group of seven rivers. This has given rise to a difference of opinion amongst scholars.

Thus Sayana includes the Ganges and the Jamuna in the group, which, according to Prof. Max Muller, is made up by adding the Indus and the Sarasvati to the five rivers of the Panjaub. On the other hand, Lassen and Ludwig hold that the Kubha must be included in the group at the cost of the Sarasvati. This shows that we are not on a safe ground in supposing that the expression "seven rivers" once meant what is, by nature, "the land of five rivers." The expression *sapta sindhavah* occurs in about a dozen places in the Rig-Veda, and in five of these it distinctly denotes the seven rivers set free by Indra along with the release of cows or the recovery of dawn (I, 32, 12; II, 12, 3 and 12; IV, 28, 1, &c.); and for reasons given above, we cannot suppose that they represent any terrestrial rivers in these passages. In the remaining cases, there is not a single instance where the expression may be said to decisively denote only the terrestrial rivers, nay, it is more likely that celestial rivers are referred to everywhere by the expression of *sapta sindhavah*. I do not mean to say that *sapta sindhavah*, *sapta pravatah*, or *sapta sravatah* can in no case denote any terrestrial, rivers. For there are three groups of seven rivers mentioned in the Rig-Veda, — the celestial, the terrestrial and the infernal. Thus in X, 64, 8, "thrice three wandering rivers" are mentioned; while the waters are said "to flow forward triply, seven and seven" in X, 75, 1. It is, therefore, clear that like the Ganges in the Puranas, the Vedic bards conceived a group of seven rivers in the heaven, another on the earth, and a third in the nether world, somewhat after the manner of the eleven gods in the heaven, eleven on the earth, and eleven in the waters (I, 139, 11; I, 34, 11; X, 65, 9). If so, we cannot say that a seven-fold division of the terrestrial rivers was not known to the Vedic bards. But, for reasons given above, we cannot hold that this seven-fold division was suggested by the rivers of the Panjaub; and then extended to the upper and the lower celestial hemisphere. The Panjaub, as remarked above, is a land of five rivers and not seven; and though we might raise the number to seven by adding to the group *any two* insignificant tributaries according to our fancy, yet the artificial character of the device is too apparent to justify us in holding, that the expression *sapta sindhavah* was *originally* suggested by the rivers of the Panjaub. We must again bear in mind that the seven-fold division of waters does not stand by itself in the Rig-Veda; but is only a particular case of a general principle of division adopted therein.

Thus we have seven earthly abodes (I, 22, 16), seven mountains (VIII, 96, 2), seven rays or horses of the sun (I, 164, 3), seven *hotris* (VIII, 60, 16), seven regions (*dishah*) and seven Adityas (IX, 114, 3), seven *dhitis* or devotions (IX, 8, 4), seven sisters or *maryadah* (X, 5, 5-6), and possibly seven and seven gods (X, 55, 3), in the, Rig-Veda; while in the later Sanskrit literature we have the seven heavens, seven earths, seven mountains, seven oceans and seven nether worlds. This seven-fold division is also found in other Aryan mythologies, as, for instance, in the Avesta, where the earth is said to be divided into seven Karshavares (Yt. X, 16 and 64), and in the Greek mythology, which speaks of the seven layers of heaven over one another. It follows, therefore, that the seven-fold division must be traced back almost to the Indo-European period; and if so, we cannot maintain that the seven-fold division of waters, which is only a particular case of the general principle, was suggested by the rivers of the Panjaub, for, in that case, we shall have to make the Panjaub the home of the Aryans before they separated. But if the rivers set free to flow *up* by Indra are not terrestrial and if the expression *sapta sindhavah* was not originally suggested by the rivers of the Panjaub, it may be asked how we account for the number of rivers and the origin of the phrase *Hapta-hindu* occurring in the Avesta.

The true key to the solution of the question will be found in the simultaneous release of waters and light effected by Indra after conquering Vritra. In II, 12, 12, Indra, who caused the seven rivers to flow, is described as *sapta-rashmih*, or seven-rayed, suggesting that seven rays and seven rivers must have, in some way, been connected. We have also seen that the waters and the sun are said to move at the same time in the Parsi scriptures. If so, what can be more natural than to suppose that the seven suns required seven horses or seven aerial rivers to carry them over the sky, much in the same way as Dirghatamas is said to have been borne upon waters in I, 158, 6? Again according to the legend of Aditi, there were seven suns or month-gods located in seven different regions and producing seven months of sun-shine of different temperatures.

But how could the seven suns move in seven different parts of heaven except by the agency of seven different aerial rivers coming up from the nether world, each with its own sun? In short, when the close connection between waters and light is once established, it is not difficult to perceive why the waters and the light are each said to be seven-fold.

The seven celestial rivers are expressly mentioned in the Rig-Veda (IX, 54, 2), and the flowing forth of the rivers and the appearance of the dawn on the horizon are described as simultaneous in many passages, some of which have been already referred to above. Neither the Storm theory nor the geography of the Panjaub, satisfactorily accounts for the simultaneous happening of these events; and so long as this difficulty is not solved, except by the Arctic theory and the cosmic circulation of aerial waters, we cannot accept the hypothesis of Western scholars referred to above, howsoever eloquently expounded it may be.

As regards the origin of the phrase *Hapta-hindu*, which is believed to denote India in the Avesta, I think, we can explain it by supposing that the expression *sapta sindhavah* was an old one, carried by the Aryans with them to their new home, and there applied to new places or countries, just as the British colonists now carry the old names of their mother country to their new places of settlement. *Hapta-hindu* is not the only expression which occurs in the Avesta in the enumeration of the Aryan countries. We have, Varena, Haetumant, Rangha and Harahvaiti in the list, which are the Zend equivalents of Varuna, Setumat, Rasa and Sarasvati.

But it is never argued from it that the Vedic deity, Varuna, was so named from the country called Varena by the worshippers of Mazda; and the same may be said of Rasa and Sarasvati. Rasa and Sarasvati sometimes denote the terrestrial rivers even in the Rig-Veda. But there is ample evidence to show that they were originally the aerial rivers. It is, therefore, more natural to hold that all these were ancient mythological names brought with them by the Aryan settlers to their new home and there applied to new places or objects.

There are places in Burma which are named Ayodhya, Mithila, &c., and this is explained on the ground that they were so named by the Indian settlers in Burma after the well-known places in their native land. There is no reason why the same theory should not be applied in the case of *Hapta-hindu*, especially when we see that the rivers set free by Indra by slaughtering Vritra cannot but be celestial.

It will be seen from the foregoing discussion that the true nature and movements of waters released by Indra from the grasp of Vritra has been misunderstood from the days of the most ancient Nairuktas, or, we might say, even from the days of the Brahmans.

There are passages in the Rig-Veda where Pushan is said to cross the upper celestial hemisphere in boats; but the Ashvins and Surya are generally described as traversing the heaven in their chariots. This led the ancient Nairuktas to believe that the upper celestial hemisphere was not a seat of aerial waters, and that when Indra was described as releasing waters by slaughtering Vritra, the waters referred to could not but be the waters imprisoned in the rain-clouds, the seven rivers set free to flow by killing Vritra were similarly understood to be the rivers of India, like the Ganges, the Jamuna, &c., while the piercing of the mountains was explained away by distorting or straining the meaning of such words as, *parvata*, *giri*, &c., as stated above.

It was at this stage that the subject was taken in hand by Western scholars who, taking their cue from the *Hapta-hindu* of the Avesta eloquently advanced the theory that the seven rivers, set free by Indra, were the rivers of the Panjaub. This explanation, when first started, was regarded as an important historical discovery; and so it would have been, if it had been a real fact. But, as pointed out above, the Panjaub is, by nature, a land of five rivers and not seven; and it is so described in the Vajasaneyi Samhita. It is also evident that as the seven rivers set free to flow by Indra, were released simultaneously with the dawn, they could not be the rivers of the Panjaub. We do not mean to say that the Panjaub was not an Aryan settlement at the time when the Vedic hymns were sung, for the rivers of the Panjaub are expressly mentioned in the Rig-Veda. But the rivers of the Panjaub were not the seven rivers mentioned in the Vedas; and if so, a new explanation of the Vritra legend becomes necessary, and such an explanation is furnished only by the theory of the cosmic circulation of aerial waters or rivers through the lower and the upper world, carrying along with them the sun, the moon and the other heavenly bodies.

We can now very well explain how Vritra, by stretching his body across, closed the passages in the mountainous ranges (*parvatas*), which, on the analogy of mountains usually seen on the horizon, were believed to lie between the upper and the lower world; and how the waters, and with them the sun and the dawn, were prevented from coming up from the nether world for a long time in the Arctic home of the ancestors of the Vedic bards. Another point elucidated by the present theory is the four-fold character of the effects of Indra's conquest over Vritra a point which has been entirely neglected by ancient and modern Nairuktas, not because it was unknown but because they were unable to give any satisfactory explanation of the same, except on the hypothesis that different effects have been confounded with one other by the poets of the Rig-Veda. But the theory of the cosmic circulation of aerial waters, a theory which is also found in the mythology of many other nations, now clears up the whole mystery. If Indra is described as the leader or the releaser of waters (*apam neta*, or *apam srashta*), the waters do not mean the waters in the clouds, but the waters or the watery vapours: which fill the universe, and formed the material out of which the latter was created.

In other words, the conquest over waters was something grander, something far more marvellous and cosmic in character than the mere breaking up of the clouds in the rainy season; and under these circumstances it was naturally considered to be the greatest of Indra's exploits, when, invigorated by a hundred nightly Soma sacrifices, he slew with ice the watery demon of darkness, shattered his hundred autumnal forts, released the waters or the seven rivers upstream to go along their aerial way and brought cut the sun and the dawn, or the cows, from their place of confinement inside the rocky caves, where they had stood still since the date of the war, which, according to a Vedic passage, hitherto misread and misunderstood, commenced in higher latitudes every year on the 40th day of *Sharad* or autumn and lasted till the end of winter. It is not contended that Indra had never been the god of rain.

There are a few passages in the Rig-Veda (IV, 26, 2; VIII, 6, 1), where he is expressly mentioned as sending down rain, or is compared to a rain-god. But as Vritra-han or the killer of Vritra and the releaser of waters and the dawn, it is impossible to identify him with the god of rain.

The story; of the release of captive waters is an ancient story for Vritra appears as Orthros in the Greek mythology, and Vritra-han, as Verethraghna, is the god of victory in the Parsi scriptures. Now this Vritra-han may not have been originally the same as Indra, for the word *Indra* does not occur in European Aryan languages, and it has, therefore, been suggested by some comparative mythologians that the conquest of waters, which was originally the exploit of some other Aryan deity, was probably ascribed to Indra in the Vedic mythology, when Indra became the principal deity in the Vedic pantheon.

The fact that Tishtrya, and not Verethraghna, is said to be the releaser of waters and light in the Avesta, lends some support to this theory. But whichever view we adopt, it does not affect the conclusion we have come to above regarding the true explanation of the Vritra legend. Clouds and rain cannot constitute the physical basis of the legend, which is evidently based on the simple phenomenon of bringing light to the people who had anxiously waited for it during the darkness of the long night in the Arctic regions; and it is a pity that any misconception regarding Vedic cosmography, or the nature of waters and their cosmic movements should have, for sometime at least, stood in the way of the true interpretation of this important legend.

Indra may have become a storm-god afterwards; or the conquest over Vritra, originally achieved by some other deity, may have come to be ascribed to Indra, the raingod in later times. But whether the exploits of *Vritra-han* were subsequently ascribed to Indra, or whether Indra, as the releaser of captive waters, was afterwards mistaken for the god of rain, like Tishtrya in the Avesta, one fact stands out boldly amidst all details, *viz.*, that captive waters were the aerial waters in the nether world, and that their captivity represented the annual struggle between light and darkness in the original home of the Aryans in the Arctic region; and if this fact was not hitherto discovered, it was because our knowledge of the ancient man was too meager to enable us to perceive it properly.

4

Tilak the Pioneer of National Education

Lokmanya Bal Gangadhar Tilak was one of the architects of our freedom. He taught people that Swarajya was their birth-right. His teachings had a great impact on the minds of the people because he practised what he preached. Like many of our political leaders Tilak started his public life as a teacher because he regarded education as a powerful instrument of moulding the impressionable minds of students and of bringing about a change in our society's outlook on life.

An Idealist

It is necessary to study how Tilak's mind was moulded and how and why later on he took this decision to become a teacher. During his childhood his father Gangadhar Shastri, made him recite Sanskrit and Marathi verses, which sharpened his memory. During his school days, he developed a special liking for Mathematics. His sharp intellect prompted him to study the basic principles of different subjects, instead of just preparing for examinations. After passing the Matriculation examination, Bal Gangadhar Tilak joined Deccan Collage in Pune. As he was staying in the college-hostel, he could take the advantage of the college library and read books by eminent writers and thinkers on different subjects. He was also greatly influenced by the teaching of Prof. Chhatre, who inspired him to study the fundamentals of Mathematics. He offered Mathematics as his principal subject for the

B.A. examination. Tilak formed a close friendship with his classmate Gopal Ganesh Agarkar who was a student of philosophy.

Tilak and Agarkar were idealist youths who were restless owing to the degenerate condition of their country. They were greatly impressed by the efforts made by Justice Mahadev Govind Ranade for enlightening the society through institutions like Vasant Vyakhyana Mala, and Sarvajanik Sabha. Tilak and Agarkar were also impressed by the writings of a young, powerful writer, Vishnu Shastri Chiplunkar, who appealed to people to develop a sense of self-respect, instead of imitating the British rulers. Tilak and Agarkar had heated discussions about the future course of action in life. Unlike most of their contemporaries, these two young idealists decided not to join Government service and instead work for the uplift of their country. Tilak argued that it was necessary to start political work first, while Agarkar argued that they should first strive to bring about reforms in society, and then start political work. After long and heated discussions, these two young idealists took the decision to work on the common platform of education.

Both of them realized that it was necessary to educate the people in general and the youths in particular before working for either social reforms or the political movement. After taking this bold decision, Tilak and Agarkar along with Vishnu Shastri Chiplunkar decided to start a High School. Shri. Vaman Shivram Apte, an eminent Sanskrit Scholar, and V.B.Namjoshi-a young idealist who was also a realist, also joined the trio. Starting of the New English School was an event which shook the student world of Pune, and as the young teachers proved their ability, the response both of the students and their guardians became more and more enthusiastic.

The trio, Chiplunkar, Agarkar and Tilak were not content with just their work as teachers. They were searching fresh fields and new pastures. They decided to undertake the work of educating the people and launched two news-papers-'Kesari' in Marathi and 'Mahratta' in English in January 1881. The editorials in Kesari were written in a direct and simple style and the editor never lost sight of the main purpose of educating public opinion. The profession of journalism has its trials. Tilak and Agarkar as editors championed the cause of the ruler of Kolhapur. They however wrote something which was challenged in the court and as the young editors could not produce evidence supporting their statements, they were sentenced to three months' imprisonment.

Tilak and Agarkar boldly accepted the punishment and their prestige as editors rose, in society, During this period of imprisonment, Tilak and Agarkar picked up the thread of their discussions in college and realized that the gap between their views was widening. Tilak made a fervent plea for political activity while Agarkar was equally emphatic about the need for social reforms. After their release from prison, Tilak and Agarkar once again devoted themselves to educational work, while carrying out their responsibility as editors. The next step in the field of education was the founding of the Deccan Education Society in 1884. This gave an institutional base to the educational effort, the next step of which was the starting of Fergusson College in January, 1885. The statement made on the occasion of the establishment of the Deccan Education Society, throws light on the ideological position of Tilak, Agarkar, Apte and their colleagues. It reads as follows:

> *"We have undertaken this work of popular education, with the firmest conviction and belief that of all agents of human civilization, Education is the only one that brings about material, moral and religious regeneration offallen countries, and raises them up to the level of the most advanced nations by slow and peaceful revolutions."*

Prin. Apte gave evidence before the Education Commission presided over by William Wilson Hunter on 9th September 1882. His views were representative of the point of view of his colleagues in the Deccan Education Society. There was a strong plea for an indigenous agency for educational effort.

It was also stated that greater opportunities for collegiate and university education should be given to the students coming from those sections of society which had a tradition of learning. The ground for this demand was that through this enlightened class education would percolate to other strata of society. This view was in sharp contrast with the view expressed by Jyotirao Phule, the great social reformer, that it was the primary responsibility of the Government to give education for seven years to students from all sections of society.

He argued that the more intelligent students would then take advantage of the facilities for higher education. Phule made a fervent plea for equal opportunities for learning to all and said that the level of enlightenment of the entire society must be raised and education should not become the monopoly of the chosen few. Phule showed a progressive vision but his plea was not accepted by the Government.

It was evident that Apte and Tilak, who came from families with a tradition of learning, did not understand the aspirations of the masses and putforth the elitist point of view which perpetuated social inequality and gave special advantages to the so-called higher communities.

Due to differences among the Life-Members of DE Society Tilak resigned from the Deccan Education Society and Fergusson College, but he continued his vocation as a teacher.

He started conducting Law Classes for the High Court Pleader's examination. Tilak had passed the LL.B. exam. with merit and owing to his analytical mind, he developed a rare insight in different branches of Law and particularly in Hindu Law. He elucidated the different topics in such a manner that the students, besides getting the necessary guidance for the examination, were stimulated to think in a novel and original manner.

Editor as Educator

After the parting of ways in the Deccan Education Society, Tilak took over the 'Kesari' and the 'Mahratta'. Tilak regarded the work of an Editor as a sacred vocation where it was his responsibility to educate the people and enlighten them. He felt that his sphere of activity as a teacher had widened. Tilak never lost sight of the principle that a Teacher has to remain a student for life time and that a person gets the moral right to educate others only when he has studied the subject which he is teaching or on which he is writing. He read extensively and carefully and only when he was convinced that he had fully grasped all the implications of the topic which he wanted to elucidate, that he expressed his point of view through the editorial. He first gave the information about the concerned subject, then analysed it and out of such delineation of facts, emerged his editorial comment.

It was no wonder, therefore, that the readers, on most occasions, were persuaded to accept his point of view. Tilak, who was a keen student of mathematics, was always logical in his argument and was very disciplined in his exposition of ideas. Tilak did not like stylistic flourishes and always avoided rhetoric. His style of writing was simple and direct. He explained the subject but avoided superfluous expression. His style of writing was compressed and had a masculine dignity.

He mainly appealed to the intellect of his readers rather than striving to arouse their emotions. In 1886, there was a famine in Maharashtra. Tilak first carefully studied The Famine Relief Code, published by the Government after the famine in 1872. He immediately understood the significance and the implications of the Government's Resolution. In the Famine Relief code, the Government had committed itself to certain relief measures such as distributing food grains at a cheap rate, a concession in land-revenue etc. Tilak first published in Kesari, the summary of the Famine Relief Code in Marathi. He then explained to the readers that it was the moral responsibility of the Government to implement their own decision and it was the moral right of the people to demand the relief measures, incorporated by the Government in their own Famine Relief Code. Tilak then printed a small booklet which contained the important provision of the code and, with the help of the volunteers, of the Sarvajanik Sabha, distributed the copies of the booklet in the famine affected parts of Bombay Presidency.

In the then Colaba district, when the Government prosecuted the volunteers, Tilak rushed to the Tehsil town Pen and in a hugely attended meeting of peasants, condemned the prosecution. He challenged the Government to prosecute him, because he had printed the booklet which contained a part of the G. R.-The Famine Relief Code-and that as the Secretary of the Sarvajanik Sabha, he had asked the volunteers to distribute it. The collector of Colaba district was present and he then withdrew the prosecution. Tilak thus repudiated the saying that 'he who can does, he who cannot, teaches'. Tilak taught the people to become conscious of their rights; he also acted boldly and challenged the Government. He succeeded because his action was based on the knowledge of the contents and also the implications of the Famine Relief Code.

When Tilak was teaching in the New English School and later on in Pune, his students were not adults and the classrooms were enclosed with walls. When Tilak started his work as Editor and social-worker, he had undertaken the job of educating adult people. This was a public-school for grown up persons and this school had no walls. Through his writings he reached a wide section of society. Although Tilak did not appoint any deputies, many enthusiastic young people in different towns and villages in Maharashtra read out before a group of adult audience the Kesari and particularly the editorials of Tilak. Thus communication was established between Tilak and the people. The editor became educator.

EDUCATION-AN INSTRUMENT OF NATIONAL AWAKENING

It is argued by some people that politics and education go ill together. This observation can be valid only if politics is regard as a game for grabbing power and money. If on the other hand, politics means an effort of the people to fight against injustice and to end tyranny, education forms a major part of political action. Tilak as the leader of the movement launched against the partition of Bengal by Lord Curzon, made national education a major part of the four point progamme which developed in to a nationwide movement. Tilak always regarded education as a powerful instrument of social transformation and used it as a weapon not only in the movement against Bengal Partition but in the struggle for Swaraj. I think it is necessary to describe in some details the political situation in which national education emerged as an important programme.

In 1905 Lord Curzon, the Viceroy of India, announced his decision of the 'partition' of the province of Bengal. The autocratic decision was an attack on the growing spirit of nationalism and the sense of solidarity among the people of Bengal. The sinister motives of Lord Curzon had become clear from his speeches in East Bengal wherein he made an effort to create enmity between the Hindus and the Muslims in pursuance of the imperialist policy of "Divide and Rule". However, Curzon's attempt to divide Bengal, made Bengal united. All sections in Bengal, rich and poor, landlords and tenants, young and old, moderates and extremists saw in the partition an insult to their honour and a threat to their solidarity.

The Partition of Bengal and people's protest against it might have become only a local affair confined only to the people of Bengal. But the trio of India's political leaders-Lala Lajpat Rai, Bal Gangadhar Tilak and Bipin Chandra Pal-Lal, Bal and Pal-showed great political foresight and lifted the struggle of the people of Bengal to the national plane. These three leaders converted Curzon's onslaught into an opportunity for creating national solidarity. Protests against Bengal's partition were held all over India and the people of India demonstrated their solidarity against the tyranny of the British Empire. It is, however necessary to know the difference in the attitude of the leaders who represented three different trends of thought, three different currents in Indian politics, not merely at that juncture but through out India's freedom struggle. The first trend was that of moderate leaders like Gopal Krishna Gokhale and Pherozshah Mehta, who followed only constitutional methods. These liberal leaders rendered yeoman's service to the nation during the first phase by laying the foundation of our future political movement. But theirs was the politics of the elite, only of eminent personalities with a rare ability to represent the cause of India before the British Parliament.

At the other end, there were the revolutionaries, who believed that freedom could be won only through armed struggle. Some of them had become martyrs and their supreme sacrifice had kindled the flame of patriotism in the hearts of many Indian youths. However only extraordinarily brave persons who were prepared to lay down their lives at the altar of liberty could follow this path. The moderates and the revolutionaries were poles apart from each other in their methods. However, the common people could not follow either of these groups. There was the third group of leaders-the trio of Tilak,

Lala Lajpat Rai, and Bipin Chandra Pal, who had realized that it was necessary to bring the common people of India in the freedom struggle.

They therefore placed before the nation a constructive and combative programme which would develop into a mass movement. When Bengal was partitioned, moderate leaders like Gokhale expressed their protest only through circulars, memoranda, and speeches. Aurobindo Ghosh wanted to follow the path of armed revolution. But Tilak and his colleagues, Lajpat Rai and Pal, put forth the four point programme of Swadeshi, Boycott, National Education and Swaraj. This programme enabled these leaders to involve thousands of people in this apparently modest political action. Tilak firmly believed that such a constructive and combative programme alone would arouse the uncommon strength of the common man. It must be noted that national education formed an important part of the nation-wide agitation. Tilak expressed his views on National Education, through the editorials in Kesari and through many of his speeches. Tilak never did anything in a half-hearted manner. In the editorial on the programme of boycott of foreign goods Tilak described Boycott as "Yoga". He also regarded "National Education" as "Yoga" which implied highest level of concentration, resulting in rare skills- "योग: कर्मसु कौशलम्". He expected teachers to work with a missionary zeal. In one of his speeches Tilak said that he wanted "Graduate Ramdasis" (The followers of Saint Ramdas who aroused the sense of self-respect and patriotism in people) to carry on the movement for Swaraj. Tilak expected that teachers must have love for knowledge, love for students and the ability to develop the personalities of youth is by inculcating in them the spirit of patriotism. He expected the guardians to co-operate with this effort of moulding and sharpening the new generation by making their wards accept the discipline of the novel experiment in the field of education.

Tilak expected the students to instil in themselves the virtues of courage, truthfulness, sacrifice and above all an attitude of self-reliance. He expected educationists like Prof. Vijapurkar to make bold experiments and evolve the pattern of National Education. Tilak, in one of his speeches said that learning and character must be blended so that instead of producing clerks required for the administration of

British rule, National Education would train students in such a manner that in future life they would build India as a Nation.

Tilak wrote a number of editorials in Kesari on the subject of National Education and elucidated his ideas. Tilak made a fervent plea for making Marathi the medium of instruction in Maharashtra. He observed that education imparted through the mother-tongue stimulated the thought process of students.

On the other hand, while learning through English, the students faltered because they were not familiar with that language and found it difficult to express whatever they know. As a result, many students were obsessed with the notion of fluency in English and their thinking process was dwarfed. In one of his editorials Tilak wrote, "If I had learnt through Marathi, the knowledge that I have accumulated at the age of fifty-two, would have easily been gained by me at the age of thirty."

In one of the editorials he developed the idea that knowledge was power, while in one of his speeches he developed the idea'सा विद्या या विमुक्तये'. That is knowledge which liberates the mind. Tilak said that because of the rule of the British many educated people had developed a sense of inferiority. If the right type of education *i.e.* national education was imparted to students, they would be mentally liberated and would boldly think in an independent manner. Tilak while elucidating his concept of National Education, always emphasised the need for removing the bifurcation of the life of the people and the education imparted to them. He said, "education must make people fearless, truthful and enable them to earn their livelihood with self-respect; but the purpose of the British rulers was to create a class which would help them carry on their administration by acting as a link between the rulers and the ruled.

They expected from this class not just obedience but a servility of what was taught in schools and colleges was a means of conditioning the mind of students for promoting in them a slavish outlook. The purpose of national education is just the opposite. We want a new generation of youths who would respect our nation. our religion and language."

Communicating the Message of Bhagwad-Gita

At Mandalay, Tilak used his imprisonment for the pursuit of knowledge in right earnest. He learnt two foreign languages, *viz.* French and German, in order to read the works of philosophers like Comte in the original French language. One is amazed at the long list of books read by Tilak during his incarceration in the Mandalay prison. Tilak once again felt that he would be able to play the role of a teacher of the people only if he would explain to them the message of the 'Bhagwad Gita'. To Tilak, the Gita was a perennial source of inspiration. While passing through the trials and ordeals of his life, it intensified his faith. 'Gita-Rahasya' was the quintessence of this life's message.

Tilak had not just read about Karma-Yoga in Bhagwad-Gita, he had lived as a Karma Yogi through out his life. He felt that the message of Bhagwad-Gita would inspire the people to lead a life of action in order to realize their dream of swarajya. Tilak, who because of his sacrifice and suffering, had become Lokmanya was confident that if he would communicate to them the message of the Bhagwad-Gita, they would try to follow it and strive for Swaraj. Tilak was conscious of the fact that his efforts would not bear fruit in his life-time; but the ideal of 'निष्काम कर्मयोग' "action without any expectation" as stated in Bhagwad Gita enabled him to carry on his effort vigorously, throughout his life. Lokmanya Tilak wrote 'Gita Rahasya' and in doing this he was carrying on the tradition sages-Rishis-in ancient India, whose teachings transcended the limitations of time and distance. Through 'Gita Rahasya', Tilak emerged as a teacher of teachers, and also as a guide and philosopher to many of his countrymen.

After his release from Mandalay jail in 1914, Lokmanya Tilak, who was the accredited leader of the whole India, directed his energies to the task of consolidating the political forces. His efforts were successful in the Lucknow Session of the Indian National Congress held in 1916. The last five years of his life were full of hectic political activities and he hardly had any time to give impetus to the effort of national education. He taught people the lesson that Swarajya was their birth-right and that they should strive to get it. In his speeches on the political ideal of Swarajya, he time and again referred to education as a powerful means of instilling the spirit of patriotism in youth. On 17th April 1917, Lokmanya Tilak delivered a speech at Chikodi, near Belgaum and the subject of his speech was 'My ideal of Education'. In that speech he made a fervent plea for free and compulsory primary education. He told the people that through national education, they would become conscious of their right to get Swarajya and would also realize that it was their responsibility to strive for it.

Tilak made a fervent plea for the spread of education. However, owing to his traditional mental make-up, he did not advocate the cause of women's education. He was brought up in the society dominated by men and he, therefore, felt that the primary duty of women was to look after the family and bring up children. When a female High School was started in Pune, Tilak wrote against it. He was of the opinion that if at all education is to be given to girls in schools, it must be such as would make them good mothers and efficient house-wives. His views were diametrically opposite to those of Prin. Gopal Ganesh Agarkar who wrote in his journal 'Sudharak' that there should be co-education and that education imparted to girls should not be different from the education given to boys. When there was a growing demand for women's education, Tilak said that time was not ripe for such a reform. He did not want to oppose the prevalent conservatism in Hindu society so far as women's education was concerned.

When Prof. Dhondo Keshav Karve started a residential school where widows were given admission, Tilak did not write anything in support of that effort. In 1916, owing to the efforts of Prof. Karve, the first women's University was started in Pune, Tilak did not welcome that event, which had a great social significance.

When Lokmanya Tilak went to England in 1917, with the help of Barrister Baptista, he brought out an excellent pamphlet 'Self Determination' which made a fervent plea for Home Rule in India. Tilak sent copies of this pamphlet to all the editors of newspapers in England and also to the members of British Parliament. When one of his followers asked him about this, Tilak said, "We have to educate the British people about the conditions in India and I am confident that owing to our pamphlet on self-determination, I would ensure the support of the Labour Party to our cause."

A Pioneer of National Education

Tilak had sown the seeds of the ideal of national education. After Tilak's demise when Gandhiji emerged as the leader of the freedom struggle, he gave great emphasis on national education. After the non-co-operation movement of 1920, Gandhiji asked many of his followers to dedicate themselves to the work of national education. The Gujrat Vidyapeeth at Ahmedabad, The Tilak Maharashtra Vidyapeeth in Pune and many Rashtriya Shalas were started in different parts of the India. In Tilak Maharashtra Vidyapeeth at Pune, teachers like Acharya Bhagwat, Acharya Jawadekar and others, while delivering inspiring lectures on politics, history and literature, inculcated in students a national outlook. Almost all these students participated in the Satyagraha movement in 1930. Thus the seed sown by Tilak had grown into a huge banyan tree. Tilak titled as 'Lokmanya' by the people of India, is regarded by all as one of the main architects of our freedom struggle. However, it is equally necessary for us to understand the significance of his efforts for giving a new orientation to education and developing it as an instrument of guarding our freedom.

TILAK'S VIEWS ON WOMEN'S EDUCATION

As we enter the new century, it is an appropriate time to look back and take a review of the historical changes that this country has brought in the field of education and especially women's education. Women's education cannot be thought of without its relationship with the other social aspects of women's life such as child marriage, widow remarriage, women's position in the society. In Tilak's time his contemporaries like Gopal Ganesh Agarkar, Mahatma Phule, Vitthal Ramji Shinde, Maharshi Dhondo Keshav Karve, held a different view. It will be interesting to study the reasons for such a different view.

Tilak has written editorials in his newspapers Kesari and Mahratta. Firstly he objected to the curriculum of the girls school because it was just like that of British schools. The cultural and social background of Indian girls is totally different from that of British girls, and so should be the curricula. Secondly he objected the full day school timing *i.e.* six hours a day for the girls. If necessary they should attend the half-day school, after finishing their duties in the house which according to him was their first moral obligation. His third objection for women's education was that the education given to them would help them become clerks in the British offices. If they start working in these offices they will neglect their first duty which is household work. This is most disgusting and hence should be abandoned. His fourth objection was against hasty reforms. Educating few women would not help the society, but educating the common masses would only help. Spending money hastily on women's education would be a waste if very few women get education.

All these views of Tilak about women's education came as a reaction to the extreme views of the reformists of his time.

TILAK AND MANAGEMENT OF EDUCATIONAL INSTITUTIONS

Training has been one little part of Lokmanya Tilak's commitment to Indian Social Life. There are distinctive sides to Tilak's life of which the most unmistakable is his political commitment. Be that as it may, he was a political pioneer as well as an incredible researcher and a writer. He lit up each subject he took up. In spite of the fact that Education involved just a couple of years of his open and social life, his commitment in this field is interesting as in amid the whole 20 century the nation took after the example of training he chose and imitated the administration style he claimed.

Four critical occasions of. Tilak's instructive commitment which have been considered in this paper are (i) The establishment of the New English School at Pune, (ii) The development of the Deccan Education Society, (iii) The foundation of the Fergusson College, and (iv) His acquiescence of Life Membership of the Deccan Education Society. Tilak voiced his thoughts and conclusions fundamentally through articles in Kesari and through letters composed by him to his associates in the Deccan Education Society. Give us a chance to take up these occasions one by one.

Foundation of New English School, Pune

The closing of the East India Company's regime in India was the beginning of a new era in our country. The failure of the uprising of

1857 had signified that the emancipation of our land and people was to be achieved through peaceful and constitutional means. Raja Ram Mohan Roy in Bengal and Mahadeo Govind Ranade in Maharashtra were the heralds of this new orientation. A very important aspect of this Indian Renaissance was the recognition of the vital part that education had to play in the creation of modern India. The historic debate on the type of education to be imparted to our people had already been settled in favour of the modern West rather than of the ancient East.

The verdict in favour of western rather than oriental education had not only meant the virtual suppression of the old by foreigners and christian missionaries. Such a transfer of educational power, though natural and inevitable under the circumstances, was neither necessary for all the time nor wholesome. Nation building education, national education, was what we wanted, and this could not be at the hands of foreigners and missionaries, for obvious reasons. National education, education of the entire nation to achieve national ends, education of the people, for the people and by the people, was the need of the hour.

The famous Wood's Education Despatch was released in 1854. It provided for establishing administrative machinery and colleges for training teachers. The despatch, no doubt, provided the essential framework for our educational system. It was highly appreciative of western education but it introduced a very tight bureaucratic control over the educational system in the country. The despatch appreciated the value of liberal education and education for women. Though the provisions in the despatch were good in character, in effect they proved useful to the Government and to missionaries than to the people. Govt. got an assured supply of servants. In addition as the despatch had provided for grants-in-aid to institutions the missionaries were mainly benefited because of this provision. They got grants without sacrificing their religious activities.

The good intentions expressed in the despatch regarding popular education and encouragement to Indian vernaculars remained unrealised. The despatch did not refer to universal literacy although it expected education to spread over a wider field, through the grant-in-aid system. It did not recognize the obligation of the State to educate every child under a certain age; it did not declare that poverty shall be no bar to education of the deserving. The despatch did not visualise education for leadership, or for industrial regeneration nor for the defence of the motherland. As private enterprise was often discouraged, christian missionaries were the only private agency in the field of education.

Under the above mentioned circumstances a band of patriotic and enterprising young men in Pune launched the New English School on 1 January, 1880. These young men were Chiplunkar, Tilak, Namjoshi, Apte and Agarkar. Opening of the New English School proved a new era in the educational and public life of Maharashtra.

Bal Gangadhar Tilak and Gopal Ganesh Agarkar later played a vital role in their chosen fields of Politics and Social Reforms. New English School, Pune was singular in having such eminent personalities as its founders. They looked upon education as the surest way to the regeneration of our mother land. In their view, Education was to be the means of rousing the intellect, the drooping will and the slumbering conscious of their countrymen. They kept before the people a very moderate objective of cheapening and facilitating education by starting schools and colleges. This venture was very bold and ambitious particularly in 1880, though it was considered 'mad', 'hopeless', 'criminal' and 'utopian' by Tilak's contemporaries.

The founders were too determined and too full of faith to be depressed by apathy or opposition shown by the contemporaries. Through their writings about education they created among youngsters the ideas of patriotism and national self-respect. Tilak and his colleagues achieved the success to the school project through self-sacrifice. All these men had the idealism and enterprise of the pioneers in them. At the time there was a Govt. School and a few private coaching classes in Pune. While the Govt. school was fully supported by the Govt. financing, the private classes conducted by Mahagaonkar, Bhave and others were purely conducted for financial benefits. New English School was different than these. Chiplunkar, Tilak, Agarkar and Apte were so gifted that in their own way they had other things to do than teaching. New English School was extremely fortunate in having them as founders.

A few things are worth noting here at this stage. May be due to the fact that Tilak, Agarkar and their colleagues were educated in the Deccan College where western education was imported, they never thought of going back to oriental education. They accepted what Macauley and the Wood's Despatch had professed. But the starting of New English School in Pune heralded a new movement in Maharashtra. Tilak's influence over the people was so strong that people opened schools in their towns and named them 'New English School'. People were convinced that Education was a tool towards achieving freedom of the country.

Formation of Deccan Education Society

It was essential for the success of the scheme of popular education sponsored by the founders of the New English School that they should form themselves into a corporate body to ensure continuity of effort in that cause and to win public confidence as to the stability and permanence of institutions they might establish. If the public was to be invited to contribute to funds on a scale adequate to the undertaking, the administration of such funds would have to vest in the hands of the organised body, including men interested in education and possessing influence in the Society. From the very outset the founders regarded themselves not as proprietors but as temporary trustees, who on their own personal responsibility and by their own personal sacrifices, would place the school on a firm footing, and then convert it into a public institution, accepting for themselves the status of its life-long servants. When the opening of a college was in sight the formation of a corporate body became a matter of urgency.

The earliest mention of the idea of forming a Society occurred in a report of the Superintendent of the New English School for the year 1883. He mentioned in that report that in order to establish a college and to open schools all over Maharashtra it was desirable to constitute a "Board of Trustees with a Managing Committee attached to it". These words gave some idea of the constitution of the proposed

Society. When this preliminary work was over, an application for the Registration of the Society was made on 5 August, and the Society was registered on 13 August, 1885 under Act XXI of 1860 (Societies Registration Act) of the Legislative Council of India. The Memorandum of Association stated the object of the Society to be "to facilitate and cheapen education by starting, affiliating or incorporating at different places as circumstances might permit, schools and colleges under native management, or by any other ways best adopted to the wants of the people".

The constitution of the Society as originally framed in 1884 provided for setting up three bodies to carry on the business of the Society: (1) Local Managing Boards, one for each Centre, consisting of Life-Members working at that Centre, and entrusted with the internal management of the Societies Institutions situated therein; (2) The Council of the Society for general supervision and control made up of all Life-Members in active service, and an equal number of representatives of the Patrons and Fellows of the Society; and (3) Trustees to take charge of the permanent funds and property of the Society. This constitution provided for day-to-day management of the Society's Institutions, and initiative as regards the development and extension of the Society's activities for the collection of funds for the purposes of the Society lay with the Life-Members. The Council on which Fellows and Patrons of the Society *i.e.* those contributing Rs. 200 or more, and those contributing Rs. 1000 or more respectively to the funds were represented and through which they could exert influence on the management of the Society's affairs, had powers of control rather than on initiation. The Council held the purse—strings on behalf of the Society and could use that power to exert its influence. Life-Members individually and collectively supplied the driving force to the activities of the Society.

The constitution and the working of the Board was thoroughly democratic. Every Life-Member, senior or junior, stood absolutely on the same footing as regards the right of voting and eligibility to office. On their capacity to visualise educational needs and formulate well-considered plans, as also their readiness to carry out these plans depended the progress and prosperity of Society's institutions. The founders of the New English School, Pune succeeded in setting up an altogether new standard of public duty, and made the name of a Life-Member of the Society synonymous with service, sacrifice and integrity.

The non-members on the Council had to give a word of counsel now and again, and blessings with their good wishes to any project the Life-Members had put before them. If we look at the private institutions run in Maharashtra at that time, they lacked corporate organisation and consequent lack of guarantees of permanence. They were at a disadvantage as compared to government and missionary institutions. The constitution evolved by the founders of the New English School and Deccan Education Society overcame this difficulty.

We must look at the Constitution of the D.E. Society very carefully. As Tilak, Agarkar, Gokhale and others were involved in framing it, it served as a model to institutions existing at that time as also to those which were started even at later dates. A major weakness of this Constitution, absence of the Governing Council which had a majority of Non-Life Members was pointed out by the then Government and was ultimately accepted by D.E. Society in 1898. Excepting this modification the Constitution of the D.E. Society as framed by the founders continued to function well for over 100 years.

It may be said that the founders of the New English School were influenced by a two-tier management system that prevailed in England for more than two centuries. They had the House of Lords and House of Commons. The administrators came from the House of Commons while the House of Lords had a control over the working of the Govt. Similarly the Board of Life-Members was similar to House of Commons as all the Heads of Institutions were Life-Members. The Managing Council was similar to House of Lords as they had control over the working of the Board of Life-Members. Later on the concept of General Body was also introduced. The General Body had no powers whatsoever but could express their opinion on the Balance Sheet and Income and Expenditure Statement of the Society. In addition they had the power to elect non-life-members to the General Body of the Society.

Life-Membership was a new concept introduced in the constitution of the D.E. Society. Life-Membership stood for service, sacrifice and integrity. Eventually Life-Members became centres of power in the Society. Life-Members were selected by Life-Members and they continued to be Life-Members till they retired. They had the initiative in every matter concerned with the Society and its institutions. This concept attracted the attention of all the prominent educational institutions in Pune and eventually the Shikshan Prasarak Mandali, Maharashtra Education Society, Progressive Education Society, Modern Education Society adopted the institution of Life-Members. Rayat Shikshan Sanstha, Satara and Vivekanand Shikshan Sanstha, Kolhapur which have schools and colleges all over Western Maharashtra introduced this system in their constitutions.

The system has been adopted by many more Societies all over the country. However, like the degradation of political and social systems in the country, the institution of Life-Members also deteriorated. There evolved groupis and nepotism. Lifc-Members started taking undue advantages and less work. That led to laziness among them. On the one hand life-members became a matter of envy while on the other hand a matter of ridicule. Concentration of power and initiative among the Life-Members was not liked by many non-life-members. Thinkers like Prof. A.B. Shah and Prof. G.P. Pradhan opposed the system on matters of principle saying that selecting Head-Masters or Principals only from among the Life-Members was undemocratic and it was perpetuating power in the hands of a chosen few who may not be men of efficiency and character.

By 1980 some political parties took interest in the affairs of educational institutions in Pune and Maharashtra and amended constitutions of some educational societies in such a way that the Governing Councils were now prominent in the affairs of Societies though the institution of Life-Members remained alive on paper. No doubt Life-Members are the only link between Schools and Colleges and the Management that conducts these institutions. No initiative is now left with Life-Members. However, it must be admitted that the Institution of Life-Members was a prominent administrative system in educational institutions for over a century.

The Fergusson College

When Lokmanya Tilak passed his LLB examination, he had decided to launch educational activity in Pune. He wanted to start a College but could muster enough friends to start a school only when the school started.

Because of their social-political activities both Agarkar and Tilak got popularity among the people, got new acquaintances and got donations from princely states. The atmosphere was ripe to start a College. A band of workers like Tilak, Agarkar, Apte, Gole, Kelkar and Dharap were already available for the school. Student strength also grew. Matriculation results of the School were also good. The Deccan Education Society was formed in 1884 and Life-Members were available to it as devoted workers. The time was ripe to open a college.

Teachers who had joined the New English School were efficient teachers in their own subjects; Tilak taught Mathematics and Sanskrit, Agarkar History and Economics, Chiplunkar English and Sanskrit, Apte English and Gole Physics. They were eligible to teach in Colleges also as per the prevailing rules. This impressed the teachers in Mumbai University who included Prin. Wordsworth, Oxenham, Dr. McKikan and Dr. Bhandarkar, Ranade and Telang. They were in favour of allowing the D.E. Society to open a College in Pune.

Shri. Vaman Shivram Apte represented the New English School before the Hunter Commission. He stressed the need of (i) Expanding facilities of Education, (ii) Education to be made cheaper, (iii) Improving quality of education imparted in Govt. Institutions, (iv) Independence to private institutions, (v) Freedom to institutions taking grant-in-aid, (vi) Improving education in Indian Languages, (vii) Developing Indian models of education, (viii) Developing Text-Books in India, (ix) Delegating the management of higher education to Indians. The Commission was quite impressed with this deposition. Tilak and his colleagues thought Education, if controlled and imparted by Indians would produce men of quality who would also improve the social and political life of the country. Ultimately that would lead to freedom of the country. They believed that Education was the only force that could bring about material, moral and religious regeneration of fallen countries and could raise them to the level of most advanced nations by slow and peaceful revolutions.

On 24 October, 1884 a meeting of prominent citizens of Pune was held in which the Deccan Education Society was formed. Shri. Apte suggested that opening of a College could be undertaken only when sufficient donations were received from the people. Money thus collected must be vested in the hands of those who were known to be socially and morally of a high standard. In this meeting Tilak proposed a Committee to be formed for that purpose consisting of Mandlik, Telang, Wordsworth, Waderburn, V. M. Kelkar and others. Dr. Bhandarkar in his resolution praised the work of Tilak and six other colleagues.

In December, 1884 the Syndicate of the Mumbai University recommended to the Senate that the D. E. Society be allowed to start a College in Pune and if the College worked well for a period of three years the University should grant it affiliation.

Fergusson College was opened on 2 January, 1885 in Gadrewada near Holkarwada. The D. E. Society had requested the Govt. to allow it to use Shaniwarwada, but the Govt. declined.

For some time it was decided to house the College in Budhwarwada. On that occasion Sir James Fergusson made a speech and praised Tilak and his colleagues for their efforts. However, this function proved to be futile as the foundation stone had to be shifted from Budhwarwada to the present site owned by Shirole. From 1892 the College became full-fledged as it was allowed to conduct final year B.A. class. For some time Govt. was inclined to hand-over the Deccan College to D. E. Society but these negotiations fizzled out.

Opening of the Fergusson College was no doubt a triumph for Tilak and his colleagues. The reputation of the College spread all over the country in later years. Many eminent personalities have recorded their appreciation of the work done by Tilak and others. Lala Lajpat Rai, Shriniwas Shastri and Pandit Madan Mohan Malviya have been some of them.

Tilak's Resignation of Life-Membership of D.E. Society

The Fergusson College was started in 1885. While the School and the College were making rapid progress, the internal differences among life-members began to increase. Life-members on whose hearty team-work depended the continued success and progress of the Society's institutions were divided in two opposite camps around Tilak and Agarkar.

The difference that now divided them arose partly from differing views about the management of institutions and irreconcilable outlooks upon the social and political questions of the day, and partly from incompatibility of temperament, together working to produce extreme bitterness of feeling. Tilak resigned his Life-membership in October 1890. It was a fateful decision. He cut himself off from the proud handiwork of his own and his comrades' youthful idealism and set out on the rough sea of public life. It was in the circumstances a wise decision, too, because the gulf between others and himself was too wide. It was no use wasting the energies of all in endless friction and opposition. It was the question of child-marriage that first brought the elements of discord to the surface. Not only on the question of child-marriage and enforced widowhood but on others too relating to social reform. Agarkar was a radical, advocating drastic action on the part of the individuals and the Government to root out the cankerous diseases of Hindu Society.

In the view of his colleagues, education and the consciousness of social evils it was bound to produce were the most potent instruments of social reform. They were opposed to State-action to accelerate the pace of social reform too much in advance of public opinion. Tilak's opposition to social reform legislation was particularly outspoken and continuous and this circumstance must have tended to produce estrangement between these two persons. This line of cleavage was intensified by other differences regarding the management of the school and the college. In these matters Apte, and later on, Gokhale were one with Agarkar, while Namjoshi and Dharap sided with Tilak. Whatever the grouping of other individuals, Tilak and Agarkar were always to be found on opposite sides on all important issues, and an impassable barrier of thought and feeling gradually raised itself between them.

As regards pay and earnings to Life-Members, Tilak's contention was that the principle of self-sacrifice demanded that the life-members should content themselves with the pay and family provision secured by the Society, and that extra earning should go to the Society. In case of necessity, gratuities might be given to individual life-members, but no regular outside work ought to be undertaken with a view to supplementing the ordinary salary. It were best to put a stop to outside work altogether, because it created divergent interests and imported inconvenient questions into the working of the Society. If outside work was to be allowed, however, it was necessary to rule that profits thereof shall go to the common fund of the Society.

Such a rule would secure that outside work shall be undertaken out of disinterested motives purely as a labour of love. Agarkar's views on these matters stood in sharp contrast to Tilak's. He says, "I seriously differ from him on the question of private work. He suggests that no life-member should be allowed to undertake any extensive private work without the consent of the Board. He thinks that such a restriction is necessary in the interests of the Body. Now I am not quite sure that the interests of the Body would be promoted by such a restriction. In proposing the restriction he is solely influenced by the desire that every life-member should expend the whole of his energy on the work of the institutions and that nothing should distract his mind from it. This is extremely desirable; but the restriction proposed will launch us into almost inseperable difficulties... Further, the strict rules about pay and gratuities may induce some to secretly set aside this restriction to make up their pressing wants, and some may do it for the sake of helping their friends with interested motives or without them.

Thus the Board will soon have to convert itself into a most frightful Court of Inquisition producing disgust about it in the mind of every life-member, and thus this restriction will ultimately defeat its own end .... No Body can imitate the discipline of the order of Jesuits without making important modifications in it. No Jesuit is a married man; no Jesuit has private property, nor is he allowed to make any; the Jesuits have a common mess and they lodge in a common house."

Life-members were pretty equally divided on the question at issue. It must be clearly borne in mind that the outside work that Agarkar and those of his thinking had in mind was of the literary, journalistic, political or public character. They were not pleading for liberty to engage without let or hindrance in any sort of money-making activities or business, but only in such categories of activities as are indicated above. Traditions have always been held to preclude life-members from the pursuit of business as ordinarily understood. Even private tuition for gain is considered as tabooed to life-members, and regular paid service is ruled out by the pledge of life-membership itself.

It must be remembered that three of the most conscientious and devoted men in the Society—Agarkar, Apte and Gokhale—were ranged against Tilak in the fight over principles. It is not to be imagined for a moment that they wanted to dilute the principle of self-sacrifice, or lower the standard of devotion to Society. Their own sacrifice left no room for any such misgiving. The Secretaryship of the Sarvajanik Sabha was an honorary unpaid post, and the only gain that Gokhale could have looked for in accepting it was the opportunity of serving a period of political apprenticeship under the guidance of Ranade.

For conscientious and unflagging work in the interest of Society's institutions, a greater figure than Apte could not have been found among life-members. If such men differed from Tilak it must have been from disinterested motives, and for worthy objects. They must have considered the vow of Jesuitical poverty impracticable for married men belonging to Hindu Society, with their undefined family obligations to relatives far and near, and in claiming for life-members the freedom to supplement their salaries by extra earnings they were facing the facts of the situation in a spirit of realism.

It would have been intolerable to have to place one's domestic difficulties before others and appeal to them for monetary help. A regular system of gratuities would have been most difficult to work equitably. It would have been a source of personal misunderstandings and heart-burnings. It was best to allow a fixed salary and leave to each life-member the freedom to supplement it if he liked and if he could. The Society's work must always be understood to have the supreme claim on the time and energy of everyone; but after that was satisfied, according to such energy of everyone, according to such a standard as his colleagues might apply, there was wisdom in leaving a life-member free to engage in outside work according to his lights.

To cut him off from outside work was not the most effective way of making a life-member devote himself absorbingly to the Society's interests. Devotion to academic and administrative work in connection with the Society must come from the urge of his own heart and conscience, and the compelling force of tradition and example. In opposing Tilak on the ground of principle, therefore, Agarkar and Gokhale were striving for the establishment of what was practicable and attainable. The principles they proposed for the working of the Society have stood the test of time, and that their faith in them was deep and disinterested was proved by the events of 1898. The spirit of self-sacrifice did not dry up after Tilak's leaving the Body; it flowed steady and strong and asserted itself again and again in defence of the cherished principles.

5

Tilak Views on Religion and Culture

We have now finished our examination of the topic of the first home of the progenitors of the Vedic Aryans from various outlooks of view. Our contentions, it will be seen, are not in light of the historical backdrop of culture, or on certainties uncovered by semantic fossil science.

The proof, refered to in the previous sections, for the most part comprises of direct entries from the Vedas and the Avesta, demonstrating unmistakably that the artists of the Rig-Veda were familiar with the climatic conditions witnessible just in the Arctic area and that the essential Vedic divinities, for example, the rotating Dawn, the Waters spellbound by Vritra, the Ashvins the rescuers of the tormented divine beings and Surya, Indra the god of a hundred penances, Vishnu the vaststrider, Varuna the master of night and the sea, the Aditya siblings or the seven month to month sun-divine beings, Trita or the Third, and others, are dressed with qualities which plainly deceive their Arctic birthplace.

At the end of the day, all the differential, specified in the third section as normal for the Polar and Circum-Polar districts, are met with in the Rig-Veda so as to leave most likely in regards to the conclusion to be drawn from them. A day or a night of six months, and a long nonstop first light of a few days' term with its spinning brilliant qualities, also the strangely long Arctic day and night or a year of under twelve months' daylight, were all known to the Vedic versifiers, and have been portrayed by them not fancifully or figuratively but rather straightforwardly in plain and basic words, which, however misjudged so long, can, in the light tossed upon the question by late logical looks into, be currently properly read and caught on.

Truth be told the undertaking, which I set to myself, was to discover such sections, and show how without the genuine key to their importance, they have been subjected to constrained development, or disregarded and dismissed, by Vedic researchers both Indian and remote, antiquated and current. I don't mean, notwithstanding, to underrate, on that record, the esteem or the significance of the works of Indian Nairuktas like Yaska, or reporters like Sayana. Without their guide we ought to have, it is promptly conceded, possessed the capacity to do little in the field of the Vedic translation; and I am completely mindful of the administration they have rendered to this bring about.

There is no doubt that they have done their best in explaining the importance of our hallowed books; and their cases on the thankful recognition of their administrations by future eras of researchers will ever stay unchallenged. Yet, in the event that the Vedas are truly the most seasoned records of our race, who can deny that in the light of the propelling learning with respect to primitive mankind, we may in any case find in these old records actualities and explanations which may have gotten away from the consideration of more seasoned researchers attributable to the flawed nature, in their days, of those sciences which are figured to toss promote light on the propensities and situations of the most seasoned predecessors of our race?

There is, consequently, nothing abnormal if a portion of the sections in the Rig-Veda and the Avesta reveal to us thoughts which the antiquated pundits couldn't and did not see in them; and I would ask for the peruser to tolerate this as a top priority in looking at the elucidations and clarifications proposed by me in the previous parts with the present translations of these entries by eastern or western

Vedic researchers. In any case, our decisions don't lay just on the elucidation of entries which, if appropriately interpreted, uncover climatic attributes impossible to miss to the Arctic districts; however this proof is, independent from anyone else, adequate to demonstrate our speculation. We have seen that in the conciliatory writing of the Vedic individuals and in addition in their mythology there are numerous signs which indicate similar conclusion; and these are completely substantiated by the old conventions and legends in the Avesta furthermore by the mythologies of the European branches of the Aryan race.

A conciliatory session of ten months held by the Dashagvas, or a yearly sattra of similar span, contrasted and the most seasoned Roman year finishing in December or the tenth month, are the key cases on the point; and they have been completely examined in the prior sections. I have additionally demonstrated that the information of the half-year-taxing day or night is not bound to the customs of the eastern Aryas, yet is basic likewise to the European branches of the Aryan race.

The custom saved in the Vendidad about the antiquated Iranian Paradise in the far north, so that a year was equivalent to a day to the tenants thereof, and its devastation by snow and ice covering the land under a thick icecap, again bears the most striking and relevant verification of the hypothesis we have attempted to demonstrate in these pages.

Thus if the traditions of the western Aryas point out, according to Prof. Rhys, to Finland or the White Sea as the original home of the Aryan people, the Vedic and the Avestic traditions carry us still farther to the north; for a continuous dawn of thirty days is possible only within a few degrees of the North Pole. But though the latitude of the original home can be thus ascertained more or less definitely, yet there is unfortunately nothing in these traditions which will enable us to determine the longitude of the place, or, in other words, whether the original home of the Aryan race was to the north of Europe or Asia.

But considering the fact that the traditions of the original Polar home are better preserved in the sacred books of the Brahmins and the Parsis, it is not unlikely that the primeval home was located to the north of Siberia rather than to the north of Russia or Scandinavia. It is, however, useless to speculate on the point without further proof. The Vedic and the Avestic evidence clearly establish the existence of a primeval Polar home, the climate of which was mild and temperate in ancient times, before it was invaded by the Glacial epoch; and with this result we must rest content, until we get sufficient new materials to ascertain the exact position of the Aryan home within the Arctic regions.

We commenced the book with a summary of the results of the latest geological and archeological researches regarding the history of primitive humanity and the invasion of northern Europe and Asia by a series of glacial epochs in the Quarternary era. This discussion was prefixed to the book with the object of clearing up certain misapprehensions regarding the early history of our planet based on knowledge derived from older geological works, when man was believed to be postglacial; and it will now be seen that our theory of the primeval Arctic home of the Aryan races is in perfect accord with the latest and most approved geological facts and opinions.

A primeval Arctic home would have been regarded an impossibility, had not science cleared the ground by establishing that the antiquity of man goes back to the Tertiary era, that the climate of the Polar regions was mild and temperate in interglacial times, and that it was rendered cold and inclement by the advent of the Glacial epoch. We can now also understand why attempts to prove the existence of an Arctic home by discovering references to severe winter and cold in the Vedas did not succeed in the past.

The winter in the primeval home was originally, that is, in interglacial times, neither severe nor inclement, and if such expressions as "a hundred winters" (*shatam himah*) are found in the Vedic literature, they cannot be taken for reminiscences of severe cold winters in the original home; for the expression came into use probably because the year in the original home closed with a winter characterized by the long Arctic night. It was the advent of the Ice Age that destroyed the mild climate of the original home and converted it into an ice-bound land unfit for the habitation of man. This is well expressed in the Avesta which describes the Airyana Vaejo as a happy land subsequently converted by the invasion of Angra Mainyu into a land of severe winter and snow. This correspondence between the Avestic description of the original home and the result of the latest geological researches, at once enables us to, fix the age of the Arctic home, for it is now a well-settled scientific fact that a mild climate in the Polar regions was possible only in the inter-Glacial and not in the post-Glacial times.

But according to some geologists 20,000 or even 80,000 years have passed since the close of the last Glacial epoch; and as the oldest date assigned to the Vedic hymns does not go beyond 4500 B.C., it may be contended that the traditions of the Ice Age, or of the inter-Glacial home, cannot be supposed to have been accurately preserved by oral transmission for thousands of years that elapsed between the commencement of the post-Glacial era and the oldest date of the Vedic hymns. It is, therefore, necessary to examine the point a little more closely in this place. In my *Orion or Researches into the antiquity of the Vedas*, I have shown that while the Taittiriya Samhita and the Brahmans begin the Nakshatras with the Krittikas or the Pleiades, showing that the vernal equinox then coincided with the aforesaid asterism (2500 B.C.), the Vedic literature contains traces of Mriga or Orion being once the first of the Nakshatras and the hymns of the Rig-Veda, or at least many of them, which are undoubtedly older than the Taittiriya Samhita, contain reference to this period, that is, about 4500 B.C. approximately It is also pointed out that there are faint traces of the same equinox being once in the constellation of Punarvasu, presided over by Aditi, which was possible in about 6,000 B.C. I have in my later researches tried to push back this limit by searching for the older zodiacal positions of the vernal equinox in the Vedic literature, but I have not found any evidence of the same.

My attention was, however, directed more and more to passages containing traces of an Arctic calendar and an Arctic home, and I have been gradually led to infer therefrom that at about 5000 or 6000 B.C., the Vedic Aryas had settled on the plains of Central Asia, and that at the time the raditions about the existence of the Arctic hone and its destruction by snow and ice, as well as about the Arctic origin of the Vedic deities, were definitely known to the bards of these races.

In short, researches in Vedic chronology and calendar do not warrant us in placing the advent of the last Glacial epoch, which destroyed the ancient Aryan home, at a time several thousands of years previous to the Orion period; and from what has been stated in the first two chapters of the book, it will be seen that this estimate well agrees with the conclusions of American geologists, who, from an examination of the erosion of valleys and similar other well-ascertained facts, assign to the close of the last Glacial epoch a date not older than about 8000 B.C.

We might even go further and say that ancient Vedic chronology and calendar furnish an independent corroboration of the moderate view of the American geologists; and when two independent lines of research unexpectedly lead us to the same result, we may very well reject, at least in the present state of our knowledge, the extravagant speculations of Croll and his followers, and, for all practical purposes, adopt the view that the last Glacial epoch closed and the post-Glacial period commenced at about 8000 B.C. From this to the Orion period is an interval of about 3000 years, and it is not at all improbable that the traditions of the ancient home should have been remembered and incorporated into hymns whose origin can be clearly traced to that period.

In short, the Vedic traditions, far from being contradictory to the scientific evidence, only serve to check the extravagant estimates regarding the age of the last Glacial epoch; and if the sober view of American geologists be adopted, both geology and the traditions recorded in the ancient books of the Aryan race will be found alike to point out to a period not much older than 8000 B.C. for the commencement of the post-Glacial era and the compulsory migration of the Aryan races from their Arctic home.

And not only Vedic but also Puranic chronology, properly understood, leads us to the same conclusion. According to the Puranas the earth and the whole universe are occasionally subjected to destruction at long intervals of time, the earth by a small and the universe by a grand deluge.

Thus we are told that when the god Brahma is awake during *his* day the creation exists; but when at the end of the day he goes to sleep, the world is destroyed by a deluge, and is re-created when he awakes from his sleep and resumes his activity the next morning. Brahma's evening and morning are thus synonymous with the destruction and the re-creation of the earth. A day and a night of Brahma are each equal to a period of time called a *Kalpa*, and a *Kalpa* is taken for a unit in measuring higher periods of time. Two *Kalpas* constitute a nycthemeron (day and night) of Brahma, and 360 × 2 = 720 *Kalpas* make his year, while a hundred such years constitute his life-time, at the end of which a grand deluge overtakes the whole universe including Brahma.

Now according to the Code of Manu and the Mahabharata the four yugas of Krita, Treta, Dvapara and Kali form a yuga of gods, and a thousand such yugas make a Kalpa or a day of Brahma of 12,000,000 years, at the end of which a deluge destroys the world. The Puranas, however, have adopted a different method of computation. The four yugas of Krita, Treta, Dvapara and Kali are there said to constitute a Mahayuga; 71 such Maha-yugas constitute a Manvantara, and 14 Manvantaras make a *Kalpa*, which, according to this method of counting, contains 4,320,000,000 years. The difference between the durations of a *Kalpa* according to these two methods is due to the fact that the years making up the four yugas of Krita, Treta, Dvapara and Kali are considered to be *divine* in the latter, while they are obviously human in Manu and the Mahabharata.

For further details the reader is referred to the late Mr. S. B. Dixit's *History of Indian Astronomy* in Marathi, Prof. Rangacharya's essay on *Yugas*, and Mr. Aiyer's *Chronology of Ancient India*, a book, in which the question of yugas and especially that of the beginning of the Kali yuga, is subjected to a searching and exhaustive examination. The Hindu writers on astronomy seem to have adopted the same system, except Aryabhatta, who holds that 72, and not 71, Mahayugas make a Manvantara, and that a Mahayuga is divided into four equal parts which are termed Krita, Treta, Dvapara and Kali.

According to this chronological system, we are, at present, in the 5003rd year (elapsed) of the Kali yuga of the 28th Maha-yuga of the 7th (Vaivasvata) Manvantara of the current Kalpa; or, 1,972,949,003 years have, in other words, elapsed since the deluge which occurred at the beginning of the present or the Shveta-varaha Kalpa. This estimate is, as observed by Prof. Rangacharya, quite beyond the limit admitted by modern geology; and it is not unlikely that Hindu astronomers, who held the view that the sun, the moon, and all the planets were in a line at the beginning of the Kalpa, arrived at this figure by mathematically calculating the period during which the sun, the moon and all the planets made an integral number of complete revolutions round the earth.

We need not, however, go into these details, which howsoever interesting are not relevant to the subject in hand. A cycle of the four yugas, *viz.*, Krita, Treta, Dvapara and Kali, is, it will be seen, the basis of this chronological system, and we have therefore to examine more critically what this collection of four yugas, otherwise termed a Maha-yuga, really signifies and whether the period of time originally denoted by it was the same as it is said to be at present. Prof. Rangacharya and especially Mr. Aiyer have ably treated this subject in their essays, and I agree in the main with them in their conclusions. I use the words "in the main" deliberately, for though my researches have independently led me to reject the hypothesis of "*divine* years," yet there are certain points which cannot, in my opinion, be definitely settled without further research. I have shown previously that the word *yuga* is used in the Rig-Veda to denote "a period of time," and that in the phrase *manusha yuga* it cannot but be taken to denote "a month."

Yuga is, however, evidently used to denote a longer period of time in such expressions as *Devanam prathame yuge* in the Rig-Veda, X, 72, 3; while in the Atharva Veda VIII, 2, 21, which says "We allot to thee a hundred, ten thousand years, two, three, (or) four *yugas*," a *yuga* evidently means a period of not less than 10,000 years; and Mr. Aiyer is right in pointing out that the omission of the word "one" in the above verse is not accidental.

According to this view a *yuga* may be taken to have, at the longest, denoted a period of 10,000 years in the days of the Atharva Veda Samhita. Now it is found that Manu and the Mahabharata both assign 1000, 2000, 3000 and 4000 years to the four yugas of Kali, Dvapara, Treta and Krita respectively. In other words, the durations of Dvapara, Treta and Krita are obtained by doubling, trebling and quadrupling the duration of Kali; and taking into consideration that Krita (which Mr. Aiyer compares with Latin *quatuor*) means "four" in Sanskrit literature, the names of the yugas may perhaps be derived from this fact. We are, however, concerned with the duration of the four yugas, and adding up the numbers given above, we obtain 10,000 years for a cycle of four yugas, or a *Maha-yuga* according to the terminology explained above. Manu and Vyasa, however, add to this 10,000 another period of 2,000 years, said to represent the Sandhya or the Sandhyamsha periods intervening between the different *yugas*. Thus the Krita age does not pass suddenly into Treta, but has a period of 400 years interposed at each of its ends, while the Treta is protected from the contact of the preceding and the succeeding yuga by two periods of 300 years each, the Dvapara of 200 and the Kali of 100 years.

The word *Sandhya* denotes the time of the dawn in ordinary literature; and Mr. Aiyer points out that as the period of the dawn and the gloaming, or the morning and the evening twilight, is each found to extend over three out of thirty *ghatis* of a day, so one-tenth of the period of each yuga is assigned to its *Sandhya* or the period of transition into another yuga: and that these supplementary periods were subsequent amendments. The period of 10,000 years for a cycle of the four yugas is thus increased to 12,000, if the *Sandhya* periods are included in it, making Krita comprise 4800, Treta 3600, Dvapara 2400 and Kali 1200 years. Now at the time of the Mahabharata or the Code of Manu, the Kali yuga had already set in; and if the yuga contained no more than 1000, or, including the Sandhyas, 1200 *ordinary* years, it would have terminated about the beginning of the Christian era.

The writers of the Puranas, many of which appear to have been written during the first few centuries of the Christian, era, were naturally unwilling to believe that the Kali yuga had passed away, and that they lived in the Krita yuga of a new Maha-yuga; for the Krita yuga meant according to them a golden age, while the times in which they lived showed signs of degeneration on all sides. An attempt was, therefore, made to extend the duration of the Kali yuga by converting 1000 (or 1200) ordinary human years thereof into as many *divine* years, a single *divine* year, or a year of the gods, being equal to 360 human years. A Vedic authority for such an interpretation was found in the text from the Taittiriya Brahmana, which, we have quoted and discussed previously, *viz.*, "That which is a year is a day of the gods." Manu and Vyasa simply assign 1000 years to the Kali yuga.

But as Manu, immediately after recording the duration of the *yugas* and their *Sandhyas*, observes "that this period of 12,000 years is called the yuga of the gods," the device of converting the ordinary years of the different yugas into as many divine years was, thereby, at once rendered plausible; and as people were unwilling to believe that they could be in a yuga other than the Kali, this solution of the difficulty was universally adopted, and a Kali of 1200 ordinary years was at once changed, by this ingenious artifice, into a magnificent cycle of as many divine, or 360 × 1200 = 432,000 ordinary years.

The same device converted, at one stroke, the 12,000 ordinary years of a Maha-yuga, into as many divine, or 360 × 12,000 = 4,320,000 ordinary years, affecting in a similar way the higher cycles of time like Manvantaras and Kalpas.

How the beginning of the Kali yuga was thrown back, by astronomical calculations, to 3102 B.C., when this hypothesis of "divine years" was adopted is a separate question by itself; but not being pertinent to the subject in hand we need not go into it in this place. Suffice it to say that where chronology is invested with semi-religious character, artifices or devices, like the one noticed above, are not unlikely to be used to suit the exigencies of the time; and those who have to investigate the subject from a historical and antiquarian point of view must be prepared to undertake the task of carefully sifting the data furnished by such chronology, as Prof. Rangacharya and Mr. Aiyer have done in their essays referred to above.

From a consideration of the facts stated above it will be seen that so far as the Code of Manu and the Mahabharata are concerned, they preserve for us a reminiscence of a cycle of 10,000 years comprising the four yugas, the Krita, the Treta, the Dvapara and the Kali; and that the Kali yuga of one thousand years had been already set in. In other words, Manu and Vyasa obviously speak only of a period of 10,000, or, including the Sandhyas, of 12,000 ordinary or human (not divine) years, from the beginning of the Krita to the end of the Kali yuga; and it is remarkable that in the Atharva Veda we should find a period of 10,000 years apparently assigned to one yuga. It is not, therefore, unlikely that the Atharva Veda takes the Krita, the Treta, the Dvapara and the Kali together, and uses the word *yuga* to denote the combined duration of all these in the passage referred to above. Now considering the fact that the Krita age is said to commence after a *pralaya* or the deluge, Manu and Vyasa must be understood to have preserved herein an old tradition that about 10,000 years before their time (supposing them to have lived at the beginning of the Kali age of 1200 years), the new order of things commenced with the Krita age; or, in other words, the deluge which destroyed the old order of things occurred about 10,000 years before their time.

The tradition has been very much distorted owing to devices adopted in later times to make the traditional chronology suit the circumstances of the day. But still it is not difficult to ascertain the original character of the tradition; and when we do so, we are led to conclude that the beginning of the new order of things, or, to put it more scientifically, the commencement of the current post-Glacial era was, according to this tradition, not assigned to a period older than 10,000 years before the Christian era. We have shown that researches in Vedic chronology do not allow us to carry back the date of the post-Glacial era beyond this estimate, for traditions of the Arctic home appear to have been well understood by the bards of the Rig-Veda in the Orion period.

It is, therefore, almost certain that the invasion of the Arctic Aryan home by the last Glacial epoch did not take place at a time older than 10,000 B.C. The American geologists, we have seen, have arrived at the same conclusion on independent scientific grounds; and when the Vedic and the Puranic chronology indicate nearly the same time,— a difference of one or two thousand years, in such cases, does not matter much,— we may safely reject the extravagant estimates of 20,000 or 80,000 years and adopt, for all practical purposes, the view that the last Glacial epoch closed and the post-Glacial period commenced at about 8,000, or, at best, about 10,000 B.C.

We have now to consider how the tradition about the existence of the original home at the North Pole and its destruction by snow and ice of the Glacial epoch, and other cognate reminiscences were preserved until they were incorporated into the law-book of the Mazdayasnians and the hymns of the Rig-Veda. That a real tradition is preserved in these books is undoubted, for we have seen that an examination of the traditions preserved by the European branches of the Aryan rage have led Prof. Rhys to the same conclusion; and those who know the history of the preservation of our sacred books will see nothing improbable herein.

In these days of writing and printing, we have no need to depend upon memory, and consequently we fail to realize what memory, kept under the strictest discipline, is capable of achieving. The whole of the Rig-Veda, nay, the Veda and its nine supplementary books, have been preserved by the Brahmins of India, letter for letter and accent for accent, for the last 3000 or 4000 years at least; and priests who have done so in recent times may well be credited with having faithfully preserved the traditions of the ancient home, until they were incorporated into the sacred books. These achievements of disciplined memory may appear marvellous to us at present; but, as stated above, they were looked upon as ordinary feats when memory was trusted better than books, and trained and cultivated with such special care as to be a faithful instrument for transmitting along many generations whatever men were most anxious to have remembered.

It has been a fashion to cry down the class of priests who make it their sole profession to cultivate their memory by keeping it under strict discipline and transmit by its means our sacred writings without the loss of a single accent from generation to generation. They have been described, even by scholars like Yaska, as the carriers of burden, and compared by others to parrots who repeat words without understanding their meaning. But the service, which this class has rendered to the cause of ancient history and religion by preserving the oldest traditions of the race, is invaluable; and looking to the fact that a specially disciplined memory was needed for such preservation, we cannot but gratefully remember the services of those whose hereditary devotion to the task, we might say, the sacred religious task, rendered it possible for so many traditions to be preserved for thousands of years. Pandits might analyze and explain the Vedic hymns more or less elaborately or correctly; but for that reason, we cannot forget that the very basis of their labours would have been lost long ago, had the institution of priests who made disciplined memory their exclusive business in life not been in existence. If the institution has outlived its necessity,—which is doubtful, for the art of writing or printing can hardly be trusted to the same extent as disciplined memory in such matters,—we must remember that religious institutions are the hardest to die in any country in the world.

We may, therefore, safely assert that Vedic and Avestic traditions, which have been faithfully preserved by disciplined memory, and whose trustworthiness is proved by Comparative Mythology, as well as by the latest researches in Geology and Archaeology, fully establish the existence of an Arctic home of the Aryan people in interglacial times; and that after the destruction of this home by the last Glacial epoch the Aryan people had to migrate southwards and settle at first in the northern parts of Europe or on the plains of Central Asia at the beginning of the post-Glacial period, that is about 8000 B.C. The antiquity of the Aryan race is thus carried back to interglacial times, and its oldest home to regions round about the North Pole, where alone a long dawn of thirty days is possible.

Whether other human races, beside the Aryan, lived with them in the circumpolar country is a question which does not fall within the purview of this book. Dr. Warren, in his *Paradise Found*, has cited Egyptian, Akkadian, Assyrian, Babylonian, Chinese and even Japanese traditions indicating the existence of an Arctic home of these races in ancient times; and from a consideration of all these he arrives at the conclusion that the cradle of the *whole human race* must be placed in the circum-polar regions, a conclusion in which he is also supported by other scholars. But, as observed by Prof. Rhys, it is no fatal objection to the view we have endeavoured to prove in these pages, that the mythologies of nations, beside the Aryan, also point to the North Pole as their original home; for it is not contended that the Aryans may be the only people of northern origin. On the contrary, there are grounds to believe that the five races of men (*pancha janah*) often mentioned in the Rig-Veda may have been the races which lived with the Aryans in their original home, for we cannot suppose that the Vedic Aryas after their dispersion from the original home met only with five races in their migrations, or were divided only into five branches. But the question is one which can be finally decided only after a good deal of further research; and as it is not necessary to mix it up with the question of the original home of the Aryans, we may leave it out for the present.

If the North Pole is conclusively shown to be the cradle of the human race hereafter, it would not affect in the least the conclusion we have drawn in these pages from a number of definite Vedic and Avestic traditions, but if the existence of the Aryan home near the North Pole is proved, as we have endeavoured to do in the foregoing pages, by independent testimony, it is sure to strengthen the probability of the northern home of the whole human race; and as the traditions of the Aryan people are admittedly better preserved in the Veda and the Avesta than those of any other race, it is safer and even desirable to treat the question of the primeval Aryan home independently of the general problem taken up by Dr. Warren and other scholars. That the Veda and the Avesta are the oldest books of the Aryan race is now conceded by all, and we have seen that it is not difficult to ascertain, from traditions contained therein, the site of the Aryan Paradise, now that we begin to search for it in the light thrown upon the subject by modern scientific researches.

But if the fact of an early Aryan home in the far north is once established by indisputable traditional evidence, it is sure to revolutionize the existing views regarding the primitive history or religion of the Aryan races. Comparative philologists and Sanskritists, who looked for the primeval home "somewhere in Central Asia," have advanced the theory that the whole progress of the Aryan race, intellectual, social or moral from primeval savagery to such civilization as is disclosed by the Vedic hymns, was effected on the plains of Central Asia. It was on these plains, we are told, that our oldest ancestors gazed upon the wonders of dawn or the rising sun with awe and astonishment, or reverentially watched the storm-clouds hovering in the sky to be eventually broken up by the god of rain and thunder, thereby giving rise to the worship of natural elements and thus laying down the foundations of later Aryan mythology.

It was on these plains that they learnt the art of weaving, the products of which superseded the use of hides for clothing, or constructed their chariots, or trained their horses, or discovered the use of metals like gold and silver. In short, all the civilization and culture which Comparative Philology proves on linguistic grounds to have been common to the different Aryan races before their separation is regarded to have, first originated or developed on the plains of Central Asia in post-Glacial times. Dr. Schrader, in his *Prehistoric Antiquities of the Aryan Peoples*, gives us an exhaustive summary of facts and arguments regarding primitive Aryan culture and civilization which can be deduced from Linguistic Palaeology, or Comparative Philology, and as a repertory of such facts the book stands unrivalled.

But we must remember that the results of Comparative Philology, howsoever interesting and instructive they may be from the linguistic or the historical point of view, are apt to mislead us if we know not the site of the original home, or the time when it was inhabited or abandoned by the ancestors of our race. Comparative Philology may teach us that cow was an animal known and domesticated before the Aryan separation, or that the art of weaving was known in those old days, because the words "cow" and "weave" can be traced in all the Aryan languages. But it is now found that equations like these do not help us much in definitely ascertaining where the united Aryans lived and when they separated; while recent researches in Archaeology and Anthropology have exhibited the improbability of a Central Asian home of the Aryan races and successive migrations therefrom to European countries. The hypothesis of a Central Asian home is, therefore, now almost abandoned; but strange to say, that those, who maintain that Europe was inhabited at the beginning of the Neolithic age by the ancestors of the races who now inhabit the same regions, are prepared to leave undetermined the question whether these races originated in Europe or went there from some other land.

Thus Canon Taylor, in his *Origin of the Aryans*, confidently advises us that we need not concern ourselves with the arguments of those who assert that Europe was inhabited by the ancestors of the existing races even in the Paleolithic period; for, says he, "philologists will probably admit that within the limits of the Neolithic age, it would be possible to find sufficient time for the evolution and the differentiation of the Aryan languages." In the last chapter of the same book we are further informed that the mythologies of the different branches of the Aryan race must have been developed after their separation, and that resemblances, like Dyaus-pitar and Jupiter, or Varuna and Uranus, must be taken to be merely verbal and not mythological in their origin. In short, the advocates of the Central Asian as well, as of the northern European home of the Aryans are both unwilling to carry back the beginning of the Aryan civilization beyond post-Glacial times, and we are told that Aryan mythology and religion cannot, therefore, claim any higher antiquity.

All such guesses and speculations about the origin of the Aryan race and its civilization will have now to be revised in the new light thrown upon the subject by the theory of the Arctic home in pre-Glacial times. We cannot now maintain that primitive Aryans were a post-Glacial race, or that they advanced from barbarism to civilization in the Neolithic period either in Central Asia or in the northern parts of Europe; nor it is possible to argue that because the mythologies of the different branches of the Aryan race do not disclose the existence of common deities, these mythologies must be taken to have developed after the separation of the Aryan races from their common home. Thus, for instance, we are told that though the word *Ushas* occurs in Zend as *Ushangh*, and may be compared to Greek *Eos*, Latin *Aurora*, Lithuanian *Auszra*, Teutonic *Asustro* and Anglo-Saxon *Eostra*, yet it is only in the Vedic mythology that we find Ushas raised to the dignity of the goddess of the morning; and from this we are asked to infer that the worship of the dawn was developed only on the Indian soil.

The theory of the Arctic home, however, makes it impossible to argue in this way. If Vedic deities are clothed with attributes which are unmistakably polar in their origin,—and in the case of Ushas, the polar character has been shown to be unquestionable,—we cannot hold that the legends pertaining to these deities were developed on the plains of Central Asia. It was impossible for the Indian priests to conceive or picture the splendours of the dawn in the way we meet with in the Rig-Veda; for it has been shown that the evanescent dawn, with which they were familiar, is quite dissimilar in character to the Arctic dawn, the subject of the Vedic hymns.

And what applies to the dawn can be predicated as well of other deities and myths, *e.g.*, of Indra and Vritra or the captive Waters, of Vishnu hibernating for four months in a year, or of Trita or the Third going down in a well, or of the Ashvins rescuing or saving the gods from the temporary affliction to which they were again and again subjected.

These very names may not be found in the Celtic or the Teutonic mythology, but an examination of the latter has been found to disclose the same polar characteristics which are possessed by Vedic deities or myths; and so long as this fundamental coincidence exists between the two, it is unreasonable to contend that the mythologies of the different branches of the Aryan race had no common origin, or that the resemblances between the names of the deities are more linguistic than mythological.

The destruction of the ancient Aryan home by glaciation and deluge introduces a new factor in the history of the Aryan civilization; and any shortcomings or defects in the civilization of the Aryan races, that are found to have inhabited the northern parts of Europe in the beginning of the Neolithic age, as distinguished from the civilization of the Asiatic Aryan races, must now be accounted for as the result of a natural relapse into barbarism after the great catastrophe.

It is true that ordinarily we cannot conceive a race that has once launched on a career of progress and civilization suddenly retrograding or relapsing into barbarism. But the same rule cannot be applied to the case of the continuation of the ante-diluvian civilization into post-diluvian times. In the first place very few people could have survived a cataclysm of such magnitude as the deluge of snow and ice; and those that survived could hardly be expected to have carried with them all the civilization of the original home, and introduced it intact in their new settlements, under adverse circumstances, amongst the non-Aryan tribes, in the north of Europe or on the plains of Central Asia.

We must also bear in mind the fact that the climate of northern Europe and Asia, though temperate at present, must have been very much colder after the great deluge, and the descendants of those who had to migrate to these countries from the Polar regions, born only to a savage or nomadic life, could have, at best, preserved only fragmentary reminiscences of the ante-diluvian culture and civilization of their forefathers living in the once happy Arctic home. Under these circumstances we need not be surprised if the European Aryas are found to be in an inferior state of civilization at the beginning of the Neolithic age. On the contrary the wonder is that so much of the antediluvian religion or culture should have been preserved from the general wreck, caused by the last Glacial epoch, by the religious zeal and industry of the bards or priests of the Iranian or the Indian Aryas.

It is true that they looked upon these relics of the ancient civilization, as a sacred treasure entrusted to them to be scrupulously guarded and transmitted to future generations. Yet considering the difficulties with which they had to contend, we cannot but wonder how so much of the ante-diluvian civilization, religion or worship was preserved in the Veda or the Avesta. If the other Aryan races have failed to preserve these ancient traditions so well, it would be unreasonable to argue therefrom that the civilization or the culture of these races was developed after their separation from the common stock.

It has been shown previously that the climate of the Arctic regions in the inter-Glacial period was so mild and temperate as to be almost an approach to a perpetual spring, and that there was then a continent of land round about the Pole, the same being submerged during the glacial epoch. The primitive Aryans residing in such regions must, therefore, have lived a happy life. The only inconvenience experienced by them was the long Arctic night; and we have seen how this phenomenon has served to give rise to various myths or legends describing the struggle between the powers of light and darkness. The occurrence of the Arctic night, its tiresome length, and the long expected morning light on the horizon after some months were, naturally enough, the most important facts which attracted the attention of our primeval forefathers, and it is no wonder if they believed it to be the greatest exploit of their gods when the beneficent dawn came dawning up, after several months of darkness, from the nether world of aerial waters, inaugurating a new yearly round of sacrifices, festivals, or other religious or social ceremonies.

It was the beginning of the Devayana, when the powers of light celebrated their victory over the demons of darkness, and the Child of the Morning, the Kumara, the leader of the army of gods, walked victoriously along the Devayana path commencing the cycle of human ages, or *manusha yuga*, as mentioned in the Rig-Veda.

The Pitiyana, or the walk of the Manes, corresponded with the dark winter, the duration of which extended in the original home from two to six months. This was the period of rest or repose during which, as observed previously, people refrained even from disposing the bodies of the dead owing to the absence of sunshine. All social and religious ceremonies of feasts were also suspended during this period as the powers of darkness were believed to be in the ascendant.

In short, the oldest Aryan calendar was, as remarked by Dr. Schrader, divided into two parts, a summer of seven or ten months and a corresponding winter of five or two months. But it seems to have been an ancient practice to reckon the year by counting the recurrence of summers or winters rather than by combining the two seasons. It is thus that we can account for a year of seven or ten months in old times, or annual sacrificial *sattras* extending over the same period. This calendar is obviously unsuited to places to the south of the Arctic circle; and the Aryans had, therefore, to change or reform the same, as was done by Numa, in postglacial times, when, expatriated from their mother-land, they settled in the northern parts of Europe and Central Asia. But the reminiscence of the Devayana as a special period of sacrifices and ceremonies was tenaciously preserved, and even now it is looked upon as a season of special religious merit. We can, on this theory, easily explain why the Grihya-Sutras attach special importance to the *Uttarayana* from a ceremonial point of view, and why death during the *Dakshinayana* is regarded as inauspicious.

How the inter-Glacial year of seven or ten months was changed to a year of twelve months in post-Glacial times, and how the equinoctial division which obtained at first on the analogy of the Devayana and the Pitiyana, was subsequently altered to the solstitial one, the old meaning of the word *Uttarayana* undergoing (*Orion*, p. 25*f.*) a similar change, are questions, which, though important in the history of the Aryan calendar, are not relevant in this place; and we shall, therefore, proceed with the subject in hand. It is urged by some writers that though the worship of natural elements is found to obtain in several ancient Indo-European religions, yet its beginnings cannot be supposed to go back to the time of the common origin of the related peoples.

Dr. Schrader has ably refuted this view in the concluding pages of his book on the prehistoric antiquities of Aryan peoples; and the theory of the Arctic home powerfully supports Dr. Schrader in his conclusions. "If we put aside every thing unsafe and false," observes Dr. Schrader, "that Comparative Mythology and History of Religion has accumulated on this subject, we are solely, from the consideration of perfectly trustworthy material, more and more driven, on all sides, to assume that the common basis of ancient European religions was a worship of the powers of Nature practiced in the Indo-European period."

The fact that the Vedic deities like Ushas, the Adityas, the Ashvins or the Vritrahan are found invested with Polar characteristics, further goes to confirm the conclusion based on linguistic grounds, or common etymological equations for sky, morning, fire, light or other natural powers. In short, whatever be the stand-point from which we view the subject in question, we are led to the conclusion that the shining sky (*Dyaus pita*), the sun (*Surya*), the fire (*Agni*), the Dawn (*Ushas*), the storm or thunder (*Tanyatu*) had already attained to the dignity of divine beings or gods in the primeval period; and etymological equations like Sanskrit *yaj*, Zend *yaz* and Greek *azomai*, show that these gods were worshipped and sacrifices offered to them to secure their favour even in primeval times. Whether this worship originated, or, in other words, whether the powers of nature were invested with divine honours only in inter-Glacial times or in times anterior to it, cannot, as stated above, be ascertained from the materials in our hands at present.

But this much is beyond question that the worship of these elements, as manifestations of divine power, had already become established amongst the undivided Aryans in the Arctic home, and the post-diluvian Aryan religions were developed from this ancient system of worship and sacrifices. We have seen that the Rig-Veda mentions the ancient sacrificers of the race like Manu, Angirases, Bhigus and others, and the fact that they completed their sacrificial sessions in seven, nine or ten months proves that they were the sacrifices of the undivided Aryans in their Arctic home.

It was these sacrificers who performed the sacrifices of, the people during a summer of seven or ten months and worshipped the mutational deities with offerings in primeval times. But when the sun went down below the horizon, these sacrificers naturally closed their sessions and made their offerings *only* to Vritrahan, the chief hero in the struggle with the demons of darkness, in order that he may, invigorated by their offerings eventually bring back the light of the dawn to these worshippers. I do not mean to assert that an elaborate system of sacrifices existed in inter-Glacial times; but I do maintain that sacrifice was the main ritual of the primeval Aryan religion, and that it is a mistake to suppose that it originated or was invented only in post-Glacial times. I have dwelt at some length on the question of ancient religious worship and ritual in this place because the theory of the Arctic home very well exposes, in my opinion, the fallacious character of many of the existing views on this subject.

A people, who had come to worship the powers of Nature as manifestations of divine will and energy, who had a well-developed language of their own, and who had already evolved a legendary literature out of the Arctic conditions of the year in their congenial home near the North Pole, may well be expected to have made a good advance in civilization. But we have at present very few means by which we can ascertain the exact degree of civilization attained by the undivided Aryans in their primitive home. Comparative Philology tells us that primitive Aryans were familiar with the art of spinning and weaving, knew and worked in metals, constructed boats and chariots, founded and lived in cities, carried on buying and selling, and had made considerable progress in agriculture.

We also know that important social or political institutions or organizations, as, for instance marriage or the laws of property, prevailed amongst the forefathers of our race in those early days; and linguistic palaeontology furnishes us with a long list of the fauna and the flora known to the undivided Aryans. These are important linguistic discoveries, and taking them as they are, they evidently disclose a state of civilization higher than that of the savages of the Neolithic age. But in the light of the Arctic theory we are naturally led to inquire if the culture of the primitive Aryans was confined only to the level disclosed by Comparative Philology, or whether it was of a higher type than the one we can predicate of them simply on linguistic grounds. We have seen above that in the case of the mythological deities and their worship the Polar character of many of the deities at once enables us to assign them to the primitive period even when their names are not found in all the Aryan languages; and the results of Comparative Philology regarding primitive Aryan culture will have to be checked and revised in the same way.

The very fact that after compulsory dispersion from their mother-land the surviving Aryans, despite the fragmentary civilization they carried with them, were able to establish their supremacy over the races they came across in their migrations from the original home at the beginning of the post-Glacial period, and that they succeeded, by conquest or assimilation, in Aryanising the latter in language, thought and religion under circumstances which could not be expected to be favourable to them, is enough to prove that the original Aryan civilization must have been of a type far higher than that of the non-

Aryan races, or than the one found among the Aryan races that migrated southward after the destruction of their home by the Ice Age. So long as the Aryan races inhabiting the northern parts of Europe in the beginning of the Neolithic age were believed to be autochthonous there was no necessity of going beyond the results of Comparative Philology to ascertain the degree of civilization attained by the undivided Aryans. But now we see that the culture of the Neolithic Aryans is obviously only a relic, an imperfect fragment, of the culture attained by the undivided Aryans in their Arctic home; and it would, therefore, be unreasonable to argue that such and such civilization, or culture cannot be predicated of the undivided Aryans simply because words indicating the same are found only in some and not in all the Aryan languages.

In other words, though we may accept the result of Comparative Philology so far as they go, we shall have to be more cautious hereafter in inferring that such and such a thing was not known to the primitive Aryans because common etymological equations for the same cannot be discovered in all the Aryan languages. We have, it is true, no means of ascertaining how much of the original civilization was lost in the deluge, but we cannot, on that account, deny that some portion of it must have been irrecoverably lost in the great cataclysm that destroyed the original home. Under these circumstances all that we can safely assert is that the degree of culture disclosed by Comparative. Philology is the *lowest* or the *minimum* that can be predicated of the undivided Aryans. his important to bear this reservation in mind because undue importance is sometimes attached to the results of Comparative Philology by a kind of reasoning which appeared all right so long the question of the site of the original home was unsettled. But now that we know that Aryan race and religion are both inter-Glacial and their ultimate origin is lost in geological antiquity, it does not stand to reason to suppose that the inter-Glacial Aryans were a race of savages.

The archaeologists, it is true, have established the succession of the ages of Stone, Bronze and Iron; and according to this theory the Aryan race must have once been in the Stone age. But there is nothing in archeology which requires us to place the Stone age of the Aryan races in post-Glacial times; and when Comparative Philology has established the fact that undivided Aryans were acquainted with the use of metals, it becomes clear that the degree of civilization reached by the undivided Aryans in their Arctic home was higher than the culture of the Stone age or even that of the age of metals.

I have referred in the first chapter of the book to the opinion of some eminent archaeologists that the mete] age was introduced into Europe from other countries either by commerce or by the Indo-European race going there from outside, and the theory of the Arctic home with its inter-Glacial civilization lends support to this view. I might in passing here refer to an instance which illustrates the danger of relying exclusively on Comparative Philology in this respect. Dr. Schrader has shown that copper, at any rate, was known to the primitive Aryans; and he admits the possibility that this metal may, in isolated cases, have been employed in the manufacture of weapons like fighting knives or lance-heads.

But we are told that there are linguistic difficulties which prevent us from assuming that gold and silver were known in the primitive period. On an examination of the subject it will, however, be seen that in cases like these the philologist relics too much on his own methods or follows them too rigidly.

For instance *khalkos* (copper or bronze) is mentioned by Homer as a medium of exchange (II, vii, 472); and Comparative Philology discloses two etymological equations, one derived from the root *mei* (Sans. *me*) denoting "barter," and the other derived from the Sanskrit *kri* Greek *priamai*, meaning purchase. The Rig-Veda (VIII, 1, 5) also mentions a measure of the value called *shulka*, and, as, the word is used in later Sanskrit literature to denote a *small* payment made at a toll-house, it is not unlikely that *shulka*, originally meant a small coin of copper or bronze similar in character to the *khalkos* mentioned by Homer. Now it is true that ordinarily Greek *kh*, is represented by *h* in Sanskrit, and that if this rule be rigidly applied to the present case it would not be possible to phonetically identify *khalkos* with *shulka*. Philologists have, therefore, tried to compare *khalkos* with Sanskrit *hriku* or *hliku*.

But, as remarked by Dr. Schrader, the connection seems to be altogether improbable. *Hriku* is not a Vedic word, nor does it mean copper or bronze. Despite the phonetic difficulty, — and the difficulty is not so serious as it seems to be at the first sight, for Sanskrit *sh* is represented by *k* in Greek, and this *k* sometimes gives place to the aspirated *kh*, — I am, therefore, inclined to identify *khalkos* with *shulka*; and if this is correct, we must conclude that undivided Aryans were familiar with some metal, either copper or, bronze, as a medium of exchange. There are many other points similar in character.

But it is impossible to go further into this subject in this place. I only want to point out the reservation with which we shall have now to accept the results of Comparative Philology in forming our estimate of the degree of culture reached by the primitive Aryans, and show that when the primitive Aryan culture is carried back to the inter-Glacial age, the hypothesis that primitive Aryans were hardly better than the savage races of the present day at once falls to the ground. If the civilization of some Aryan races in the Neolithic age appears to be inferior or imperfect it must, therefore, be, as observed above, ascribed to relapse or retrogression after the destruction of the ancient civilization by the Ice Age, and the necessarily hard and nomadic life led by the people who survived the cataclysm.

The Asiatic Aryans, it is true, where able to preserve a good deal more of the original religion and culture, but it seems to be mainly due to their having incorporated the old traditions into their religious hymns or songs; and made it the exclusive business of a few to preserve and hand down with religious scrupulosity these prayers and songs to future generations by means of memory specially trained and cultivated for the purpose. But even then how difficult the task was can be very well seen from the fact that a greater portion of the hymns and songs originally comprised in the Avesta has been lost; and though the Veda is better preserved, still what we have at present is only a portion of the literature which is believed on good grounds to have once been in existence.

It may seem passing-strange that these books should disclose to us the existence of an original Arctic home so many centuries after the traditions were incorporated into them. But the evidence in the foregoing pages shows that it is a fact; and if so, we must hold that the Neolithic Aryan people in Europe were not, as Prof. Max Muller thinks, progressive, but, for the time at least, necessarily retrogressive savages working only with such residua of the antediluvian civilization as were saved from its general wreck.

But though the Vedic or Aryan people and their religion and culture can thus be traced to the last inter-Glacial period, and though we know that the degree of culture attained by the primitive Aryans was of a higher type than some scholars seem to be willing to assign to them, yet there are many points in the primitive Aryan history which still remain unsolved. For instance, when and where the Aryan race was differentiated from other human races, or how and where the Aryan speech was developed, are important questions from the anthropological point of view, but we have, at present, no, means to answer the same satisfactorily.

It is quite possible that other human races might have lived with the Aryans in their home at this time; but the Vedic evidence is silent on this point. The existence of the human race is traced by geologists to the Tertiary era; and it is now geologically certain that the gigantic changes wrought on this globe by glacial epochs were witnessed by man. But anthropology does not supply us with any data from which we can ascertain when, where, or how the human race came to be differentiated according to colour or language. On the contrary, it is now proved that at the earliest date at which human remains have been found, the race was already divided into several, sharply distinguished types; and this, as observed by Laing, leaves the question of man's ultimate origin completely open to speculation, and enables both monogenists and polygenists, to contend for their respective views with plausible arguments and without fear of being refuted by facts. The evidence, set forth in the foregoing pages, does not enable us to solve any of these questions regarding the ultimate origin of the human race or even of the Aryan people or their language and religion. We have nothing in this evidence for ascertaining how far the existence of the Aryan race can be traced back to pre-Glacial, as distinguished from inter-Glacial times; or whether the race was descended from a single pair (monogeny) or plurality of pairs (polygeny) in the remotest ages.

The traditional evidence collected by us only warrants us in taking back the Aryan people and their civilization from the Temperate zone in post-Glacial to the Arctic regions in inter-Glacial times. It is true that: Aryans and their culture or religion cannot be supposed to have developed all of a sudden at the close of the last inter-Glacial period, and the ultimate origin of both must, therefore, be placed in remote geological times. But it is useless to speculate on this question without further evidence, and in the present state of our knowledge we must rest content with the result that though Aryan race or religion can be traced to the last inter-Glacial-period yet the ultimate origin of both is still lost in geological antiquity.

I cannot conclude this chapter without briefly examining the bearing of our results on the views entertained by Hindu theological scholars regarding the origin, character and authority of the Vedas. It is a question which has been discussed with more or less acuteness, subtlety, or learning ever since the days of the Brahmans; and frond a purely theological point of view I do not think there remains anything to be now said upon it. Again, for the purposes of scientific investigation, it is necessary to keep the theological and the antiquarian aspect of the question quite distinct from each other. Yet when our investigation, conducted on strict scientific lines, is completed, we may usefully compare our conclusions with the theological views and see how far they harmonize or clash with each other. In fact no Hindu who reads a book like the present, can avoid making such a comparison; and we shall be lightening his task by inserting in this place a few remarks on this subject. According to the view held by Hindu theologians, the Vedas are eternal (*nitya*), without a beginning (*anadi*), and also not created by a human author (*apaurusheya*); and we are told that these attributes have been predicated of our sacred books from the most ancient times known to our divines or philosophers.

The whole of the third Volume of Dr. Muir's *Original Sanskrit Texts* is devoted to the discussion of this subject, a number of original passages and arguments bearing on which are there collected, including

Sayana's lucid summary in the introduction to his commentary on the Rig-Veda; and more recently the late Mahamahopadhyaya Rajarama Shastri Bodas, the editor of the Bombay edition of the Rig-Veda, has done the same in a Sanskrit pamphlet, the second edition of which is now published by his son, Mr. M. R. Bodas, of the Bombay High Court Bar. I shall, therefore, give in this place only a summary of the different views of Hindu theologians, without entering into the details of the controversy which can be studied from the above books. The question before us is whether the Vedic hymns, that is, not only the words of the hymns but also the religious system found or referred to therein, are the compositions of the Rishis to whom they are assigned in the Anukramanikas, or the ancient Indexes of the Veda, in the sense in which the Shakuntala is a composition of Kalidasa; or whether these hymns existed from times immemorial, in other words, whether they are eternal and without a beginning. The hymns themselves are naturally the best evidence on the point. But, as shown by Dr. Muir in the second chapter (pp. 218-86) of the Volume above mentioned, the utterances of the Vedic Rishis on this point are not unanimous.

Thus side by side with passages in which the Vedic bards have expressed their emotions, hopes or fears, or prayed for worldly comforts and victory over their enemies, condemning evil practices like gambling with dice (X, 34), or have described events, which on their face seem to be the events of the day; side by side with passages where the poet says that how has made (*kri*) generated (*jan*), or fabricated (*taksh*) a new (*navyasi* or *apurvya*) hymn, much in the same way as a carpenter fashions a chariot (I, 47, 2; 62, 13; II, 19, 8; IV, 16, 20; VIII, 95, 5; X, 23, 6; 39, 14; 54, 6; 160, 5; &c.); or with hymns in which we are plainly told that they are composed by so and so, the son of so and so, (I, 60, 5; X, 63, 17; 67, 1; &c.), there are to be found in the Rig-Veda itself an equally large number of hymns where the Rishis state in unmistakable terms that the hymns sung by them were the results of inspiration from Indra, Varuna, Soma, Aditi, or some other deity; or that the Vedic verses (*richah*) directly emanated from the Supreme Purusha, or some other divine source; or that they were given by gods (*devatta*), or generated by them and only seen or perceived (*pashyat*) by the poets in later times, (I, 37, 4; II, 23, 2; VII, 66, 11; VIII, 59, 6; X, 72, 1; 88, 8; 93, 9; &c.). We are told that Vach (Speech) is *nitya* or eternal (VIII, 75, 6, also cf. X, 125); or that the gods generated the divine Vach and also the hymns (VIII, 100, 11; 101, 16; X, 88, 8). The evidence of the Vedic hymns does not, therefore, enable us to decide the question one way or the other; but if the composition of the hymns is once ascribed to human effort, and one to divine inspiration or to the gods directly, it is clear that at least some of these old Rishis believed the hymns to have been sung under inspiration or generated directly by the goddess of speech or other deities.

We may reconcile the former of these views with the passages where the hymns are said to be made by human effort, on the supposition that the poets who sang the hymns believed themselves to be acting under divine inspiration. But the explanation fails to account for the statement that the Jik, the Yajus, and the Saman, all emanated from the Supreme Purusha or the gods; and we must, therefore, conclude that the tradition about the eternity of the Vedas, or their divine origin is as old as the Veda itself. Accordingly, when we come to the Brahmans and the Upanishads, we naturally find the same view prevailing.

They tell us that the Rig-Veda proceeded from Agni (fire), the Yajur-Veda from Vayu (wind), and the Sama-Veda from Surya (the sun), and that these three deities got their warmth from Prajapati who practiced lapas for the purpose (Shat. Brah, XI, 5, 8, 1 *f*'; Ait. Brah. V, 32-34; Chhan. Up. IV, 17, 1); or that the Vedas are the breathings of the Supreme Being (Brih. Up. II, 4, 10); or that Prajapati by means of the eternal Vach created the Vedas and everything else in this world; and the same view is met with in the Smritis like those of Manu (I, 21-23) and others, or in the Puranas, several extracts from which are given by Dr. Muir in the volume above referred to.

It is admitted that the Vedas, with other things, are destroyed, at the end of a Kalpa, by the deluge (*pralaya*) which overtakes: the world at the time. But we are told that this does not affect the question of the eternity of the new Kalpa by Brahma himself after the grand deluge, and by the Rishis, who survive, after minor deluges. The authority generally quoted in support of this view is a verse from the Mahabharata (Shanti-Parvan, Chap. 210, v. 19) which says, "The great Rishis, empowered by Svayambhu (the self-born), formerly obtained, through *tapas* (religious austerity), the Vedas and the Itihasas, which had disappeared at the end of the (preceding) *Yuga*." The Rishis are, therefore, called the *seers* and not the *makers* of the Vedic hymns; and the personal designation of some Shakhas, branches or recessions of Vedas, as Taittiriya, Kathaka, &c., as well as the statements in the Vedic hymns, which say that so and so has *made* or *generated* such and such a hymn, are understood to mean that the particular Shakha or hymn was perceived, and *only perceived*, by the particular Rishi or poet.

It is not, however, till we come to the works of the authors and expositors of the different schools of Hindu philosophy (*darshanas*) that we find the doctrine of the eternity of the Vedas subjected to a searching examination; and, as remarked by Dr. Muir, one who reads the discussions of these writers cannot fail to be struck "with the acuteness of their reasoning, the logical precision with which their arguments are presented, and the occasional liveliness and ingenuity of their illustrations."

They all bear witness to the fact that so far as tradition went, — an unbroken tradition of great antiquity, — there was no remembrance of the Vedas having been ever composed by or ascribed to any human author; and taking into consideration the, learning and the piety of these scholars, their testimony must be regarded as an unimpeachable proof of the existence of such a tradition, which was considered ancient several centuries before the Christian era. But though a tradition whose high antiquity can be so well established deserves to be seriously considered in our investigations regarding the character of the Vedas, yet it is, after all, a negative proof, showing, it may be urged, nothing more than no human author of the Veda has been known from times beyond the memory of all these ancient scholars.

Jaimini, the author of Mimamsa Sutras, therefore, further deduces (I, 1, 5) the eternity of the Vedas from the relation or connection between words and their meanings, which he holds to be eternal (*autpattika*) and not conventional. A word is defined to be an aggregate of letters in a particular order, and its sense is said to be conveyed by these letters following each other in a definite succession. But Grammarians are not satisfied with this view, and maintain that the sense of a word is not expressed by the aggregate of its constituent letters which are transient, but by a certain super-sensuous entity, called *sphota* (*i.e.*, manifester, from *sphut*), which supervenes the aggregate of the letters as soon as they are pronounced, and reveals their meaning. Jaimini denies that there are words in the Vedas which denote any transient objects, and as the Vedic words and their sense are eternal, it follows, according to him, that the Vedas are self-demonstrative, or that they shine, like the sun, by their own light, and are, therefore, perfect and infallible. If particular parts of the Vedas are designated after some Rishis, it does not, we are told, prove those sages to have been their authors, but merely the teachers who studied and handed them down. Badarayana, as interpreted by Shankaracharya (I, 31, 26-33), the great leader of the Vedanta School, accepts the doctrine of the eternity of sound or words, but adds that it is the species to which the word belongs, and not the word itself, that is eternal or indestructible, and, there fore, though the names of deities, like Indra and others, which are all created and hence liable to destruction, are mentioned in the Veda, it does not affect the question of its eternity as the species to which Indra and others are said to belong is still eternal. In short, Vedic names and forms of species are eternal, and it is by remembering these that the world is created by Brahma at the beginning of each Kalpa (Maitr. Up., VI, 22).

TILAK AND GANESH FESTIVALS

Tilak was maybe the main Indian political pioneer who understood the quality of the masses. He developed numerous projects so as to unite individuals. He contended that saint love is at the foundation of nationality, social request and religion. Nehru commented that Tilak was the primary political pioneer of the new India who achieved the masses and drew quality from them. In 1895 Tilak introduced the Ganapati celebrations. Ganesh is a standout amongst the most prevalent of the divinities adored by the Hindus. The Ganapati development was introduced by Tilak as a counterpoise to the Muslim celebration Muhurram in which Hindus of the lower stations partook. Till then, Ganapati celebrations had nothing of an open character. In any case, Tilak succeeded in changing a straightforward household ceremony into an open festival.

In 1894 Tilak with the assistance of the Natu siblings was in charge of making the celebration an open occasion enduring ten days with music and a sorted out parade including young men from schools, and universities. Melodies were sung in acclaim of Tilak and Shivaji. Young men were occupied with fencing and other physical activities. The Natu siblings showed them sword and single stick activities.

Stanley A. Walport watches that through the Ganapati celebrations Tilak succeeded in uniting the up to this point disregarded urban and laborer bring down classes, influencing them with political melodies and discourses, boring young fellows to walk about town in aggressor gatherings and bestowing to Hinduism a congregational character up to this point obscure to it. Amid the parades they yelled: "O Heroes of Hind" and "Love your Country as God".

Frequently the Ganapati celebrations incited the Muslim people group. Tilak composed articles in a tone which was exceptionally offense to the Muslims, calling the Hindus to refrain from going about as the bearers of the bodies of Hassan and Hussain, that the sobbing stories of the Muslims in their Muharam festivities have nothing in them that would conscious patriotism. In 1894 and 1895 Tilak held exceptional Ganapati gatherings in his own particular house at Poona and at these tunes were sung in which direct Hindus and the British government were condemned, and Tilak affirmed these tunes.

David Smith watches that the love of Ganesh was rehashed in Maharashtra by the immense autonomous pioneer Tilak. Today, the Ganesh celebration is the biggest Hindu open religious execution in Maharashtra. Yogendra K.Malik and V.B. Singh help us that Tilak's utilization to remember the Ganesh celebrations was a case of the utilization of conventional religious images to assemble the Hindus in the reason for Hindu patriotism. As per Walport, with the Ganesh celebrations aggressor Hinduism's first cutting edge framework was conceived.

Shivaji Festivals

Tilak was instrumental in reviving the memory of Shivaji and setting in motion a great national propaganda which culminated in 1895 in the celebration at the chief centres of Brahmin activity in the Deccan of Shivaji's reputed birthday. According to Tilak, the Shivaji festivals serve like manure to the seeds of enthusiasm and the spirit of nationalism. He saw in this festival a peculiar value for the whole country, and argued that it is the duty of everyone to see that this character of the festival is not ignored or misrepresented.

Shivaji festivals at times created tension between the Muslims and the Hindus. Some of the articles that appeared in *Kesari* prove this fact. But Tilak said: "The Shivaji festival is not celebrated to alienate or even to irritate the Mahomedans. [....] We are not against a festival being started in honour of Akbar or any other hero from old Indian history".

The Shivaji festivals were also attempts to consolidate Hindu consciousness and Hindu militancy. Kushwant Singh adds that every time the Ganesh and Shivaji festivals were celebrated there were Hindu-Muslim riots. Walport says that, with the revival of the Shivaji festivals the next link in the organisational chain of militant Hinduism was developed.

Shivaji as a Role Model for Violence as Higher Duty

Shivaji, the Maratha leader, provided a kind of mythological exemplar for Tilak of his ethics of violence as higher duty, whose festivals he ardently promoted, though Mahatma Gandhi considered Shivaji as a misguided patriot. In 1896 Tilak lamented the neglect of the sites associated with the life and death of Shivaji. He said: "That the place of coronation and the tomb of that great man who gave the joy of independence to Maharashtra for two centuries should have been so utterly forgotten by the Marathas is indeed a misfortune". On 24 June 1906 Tilak wrote an article in his *Mahratta* entitled "Is Shivaji not a National Hero?" He called Shivaji '*swadeshi* hero' and argued that "Shivaji is the only hero to be found in Indian history". Tilak also began the modern promotion of Shivaji, as the leader of Maratha independence in Maharashtra. He urged children to read a portion of a historical novel entitled *Ushahkal* dealing with the times of Shivaji. According to him, what makes Shivaji a national hero is the spirit which guided him throughout and not his deeds as such. But history tells us that Shivaji treacherously murdered Afzal Khan. Ivan Strenski reminds us that Tilak's failure to bring about a method of controlled use of force must be seen at least partly as a failure of his political mythology. In a word, the myth of Shivaji sent all the wrong messages to those who might have wished for an ethic of justifiable use of force. Moreover, knowing about other ambivalent features of Tilak's political behaviour, one might conclude that Tilak chose the Shivaji myth precisely *because* it was ambivalent: it permitted him to appeal to chivalrous and heroic elements of the Maratha leader's lofty character, while at the same time permitting him to trade upon some of Shivaji's unsavoury qualities.

Strenski argues that Shivaji's killing of the Mughal general Afzal Khan raises many ethical questions. The 'great chivalric hero' Shivaji arrived with concealed deadly weapons to meet Afzal Khan. At his first opportunity, Shivaji murdered Afzal Khan on the very spot where they had agreed to talk peace. Walport describes the murder of Afzal Khan as follows:

To all outward appearances clad innocently enough, Shivaji approached the Muslim in his plain cloth shirt, but under it he wore a vest of mail, and concealed in his right sleeve was a scorpion-shaped dagger, while the finger tips of his left hand were sheathed with metal tiger claws. The embrace with which he greeted Afzal evoked the death-pang outcry from the Muslim.

What followed was the massacre of Afzal Khan's entire retinue. Now leaderless, the Mughal army dispersed and Shivaji won what Marathi patriots have celebrated as a great victory – a victory won by duplicity and deception. Shivaji's failure to keep his solemn word make him seem cowardly and dishonourable, little better than a sneak thief. Put on to the balance with the rest of Shivaji's deeds, it weighs heavily against permitting any honest reader to see in him an honourable man. Hence, says Strenski, Shivaji cannot be a role model for anyone who wishes to found an ethic of the principled or controlled use of violence.

It has been discovered that many years prior to the killing of Afzal Khan, Shivaji used the pretext of marriage to wrest control of a territory. After promising to marry the daughter of Chandra Rao More, the ruler of Javli, he killed More and took over Javli. Strenski says: "some of Tilak's own most notorious public deeds seem to indicate that his philosophy of political action was informed by the very moral ambivalence that characterises the myth of Shivaji".

Anti Cow-Killing Societies

Tilak started and used Anti-Cow-Killing Society, which in its original form was a religious movement founded on the fact that the Hindus regard the cow as a sacred animal. Unfortunately, his Anti Cow-Killing Society was regarded as a direct movement to provoke Muslims. Tilak did not take part in any anti-cow killing movement as such, but took advantage of the ill-feeling between the Hindus and Muslims for which this movement was a symptom. Tilak took a prominent part in inflaming the minds of Hindus against the Muslims. In several of his articles in *Kesari* he upheld the view that in the anti-cow-killing riots, as in all other outbreaks, the Musalmans were the aggressors. He praised the spirit in which the Hindus had stood up to their assailants when attacked and blamed those who held that when assailed by Muslims the Hindus should flee.

Gymnastic Societies

Tilak maintained that unless Hindus learned to employ force they must expect to be impotent witness of the gradual downfall of their ancient institutions. Therefore, he proceeded to organise Gymnastic Societies in which physical training and the use of more or less primitive weapons were taught in order to develop the martial instincts of the rising generation. The Natu brothers were recognised leaders of Hindu orthodoxy. They carried Tilak's propaganda to schools and colleges proclaiming that unless they learned to employ force the

Hindus must expect to be impotent witnesses of the gradual downfall of all their ancient institutions.

His Gymnastic Societies sometimes resorted themselves into juvenile bands of dacoits to swell the coffers of *swaraj*. Young Hindus were taught to use arms and induced to believe it to be their duty to employ them against the enemy. The teaching which he gave or caused to be given to the members of the said societies was of such an evil and demoralising nature that with his approbation the members of some such societies formed themselves into bands of robbers who committed murder and robbery with the object of obtaining money to pursue Tilak's political campaign.

Extremist Journalism

Tilak started two newspapers *Kesari* and *Mahratta*. He wrote incriminating articles to encourage terrorism. In several of his writings he spoke of the cheapness of bombs and the economy with which they could be manufactured. He described the bomb as a charm and an amulet and a legitimate weapon of political reform. He even considered terrorism as an expression of patriotism. He said: "There is an excess of patriotism at the root of the bombs in Bengal". He went so far as to say that the Bengalee murders were 'beneficent murders' so that, in his opinion, there might be a beneficent murderer.

Tilak used his newspapers to incite the Hindus to assert their rights. He vilified the Muslims and the British.

From June through August of 1902, *Kesari* ran a highly provocative series of nine editorials entitled 'Guerrilla Warfare'. Sometimes *Kesari* contained articles on methods of the Russian Revolutionaries and the cult of the bomb in Bengal. He openly advocated Russian methods of retaliation. Writing in *Kesari* on 16 July 1907 he exhorted Indians to follow the Russian methods of political agitation. Tilak also wrote some articles proposing to the government to make gymnastics a compulsory subject in schools

In the *Kesari* of 28 May 1907 he exhorted Indian leaders to emulate the example of Russian democrats in their methods of political agitation. He also spoke of how the Russians managed to evade press censorship. On 27 July 1907 Tilak wrote in *Kesari*: "We find in Mr. Savarkar's book a true echo of the thoughts of Mazzini, his secret and the open attempts to bring about the unification of Italy"; "We find in Mazzini's writings a clear enumeration of the noble principles of democratic politics". When Tilak began *Kesari* and *Mahratta* he had stated that the aim of the two newspapers would be to give a fearless account of the existing condition in the country, to give reviews of Indian books and to give correct estimates of political affairs in Britain. But as is evident, his columns went beyond this scope and promoted extremism and militancy. They became vehicles for his radical political views and ethics of violence.

Militant Activities

Tilak was the founder of the militant revolutionary school in the national movement. He seems to have had connections with the secret societies at Nasik, Bengal and elsewhere. He felt himself strong to capture the Congress organisation in 1907, though it was not successful. The fight between the Moderates and the Extremists carried on in the political arena led to a split in the Indian National Congress. The extremist founded a party of their own. But Tilak said that the extremist of today will be the moderates of tomorrow just as the moderates of today were extremists yesterday. In 1907 at Surat, Tilak and his revolutionary group were expelled from the Congress for their radicalisation of Indian politics, which included also Aurobindo Ghose. The rift was only healed in 1914 when Tilak finalised a pact with the Muslim League for a joint front against the British.

It has been argued that in the murder of Walter Charles Rand and Charles Egerton Ayerst at Nasik, the assassins were only giving effect to Tilak's teachings. He played a leading role in inflaming the minds of the Hindus against the Muslims. During the cow-killing agitation of 1893, which caused disturbances throughout the country and much loss of life and property, He thus showed himself as an open advocate of violence and the cult of physical force.

Sometimes he advocated insurrection and argued that the Boer system of warfare which had been successful against the British, was that which had been adopted by Shivaji against the Muslims. In 1908

Tilak was tried for sedition because of an attempt on the life of Kingsford, a British judge at Muzaffarpur. Though the intention was to murder Kingsford, the assassins missed the target and two ladies were killed. Tilak in his writings supported the bomb throwers. This bomb outrage offered the government a golden chance to arrest Tilak. Tilak was sentenced for six years in prison. Tilak was convicted for inciting disaffection against the British in his writings in Marathi. But he claimed that the English renderings were defective. The trial ended in his incarceration and he was sent to Mandalay (Myanmar) and it was there that he composed his influential commentary on the *Gita* – the *Gitarahasya.*

Anti-Muslim Attitude

Tilak played a prominent part in inflaming the minds of the Hindus against the Muslims. Between 1880 and 1890 throughout India there was an evident antipathy between Hindus and Muslims. There were numerous riots and encounters between the members of the two faiths in many parts of the county. He promoted Ganapati festivals, in the first place, to prevent people from taking part in the Muslim festival Muharram. He was accused of inciting the Hindus to assert their rights to play music in passing before mosques. He even called the Muslims a savage race. He said: "even a savage race like the Mohammedans did not disarm the Hindus while exercising their imperial sway over India".

In High Court of Justice, Kings Bench Division accused Tilak of several crimes. For example, in 1893 during the Hindu-Muslim riots in Bombay Tilak took advantage of the situation to stir up the feeling of the Hindus against the Muslims. He was accused of using the Anti-Cow Killing Societies as a means to provoke the Muslims. According to the report of the Bombay government on 16 July 1918, on the occasion of Shivaji's coronation festival, Tilak presided at a lecture on conscription. In his speech he called the army a mercenary which consisted of Muslims and foreigners. It has been observed that basically, Tilak's anti-Muslim attitude manifested itself in four things: the question of playing music before the mosques, the Ganapati celebrations, the Shivaji movement and the Anti-Cow Killing Societies.

AntiChristian Attitude

Tilak saw Christianity as an enemy of Hinduism. He said: "Now I turn to the forces that are arrayed against us. There are mainly two forces of (1) science and (2) Christianity. If our religion is threatened with any hostile criticism, it comes from these two". Once he took tea in a Christian missionary school and accepted to do penance for it.

Tilak was vehemently opposed to the so-called conversion activities of the Christians. When Pandita Ramabai, a great Sanskrit scholar who became a widow, converted to Christianity and then set up *Sharada Sadan* for educating destitute high-caste widows, Tilak alleged that it was being covertly used to promote conversion to Christianity.

Tilak never really favoured social reforms. On 30 July 1907 he wrote in *Kesari* against Christian involvement in social reform and human rights issues.

He said: Though the correspondence with regard to the abolition of the customs of dedicating minor girls to the gods at Jejuri and Savantwadi is carried on under the leadership of Dr.Bhandarkar, it is the Missionaries who are as a matter of fact at the bottom of the whole affair.

It was they who first brought to the notice of Government that such girls led an immoral life after attaining puberty and that the existing statutory resolutions were quite inadequate to remedy the [sic] evil. [....] It is not at all possible for the people to believe that the above suggestion of the Missionaries originated from disinterested motives. [....] Our hypocritical Missionaries do not seem to know that immorality is not a criminal offence in England and that the value of the chastity of women can be estimated there in damages. The missionaries needlessly interfered in the matter.

Again, referring to Christianity Tilak said: "Our enemies are fast disappearing before the teachings of modern science, take courage and work hard for the final triumph". He envisaged a time when, instead of Christians preaching Christianity in India, Hindus will see their preachers proclaiming *Sanatana Dharma* (Eternal Religion) all over the world.

Critical Attitude towards Buddhism and Jainism

Tilak did not view benevolently the Buddhists and the Jains of India. He praised Adi Sankara of Kaladi who aggressively fought these two religions. Tilak says: "Buddhism flourished and attacks were made on Hindu religion by Buddhists and Jains. After 600 years of chaos rose one great leader, Shankaracharya and he brought together all the common philosophical elements for our religion and proved and preached them in such a way that Buddhism was swept away from the land".

INFLUENCE ON THE HINDUTVA MOVEMENT

In Tilak, Hindu religion invaded the domain of politics. He was an icon of religio-centric politics in his time. But he was eclipsed by Gandhi in the leadership of the Congress Party. This political displacement of Tilak corresponded with what *seemed* the virtually final eclipse of his reading of the *Gita* as well. But it was not so. On 30 January 1948 Nathuram Godse (1912-1949) fired three shots at point blank range at Gandhi. The assassin after firing the shots raised his hand with the gun and called for the police. He voluntarily surrendered to the authorities. The Hindu Mahasabha celebrated the event by distributing sweets. Godse later said that he had done his duty like Arjuna in the Mahabharata whom Krishna advised to kill his own relatives because they were evil. He had also read Tilak's writings.

Godse exhibited a surprisingly serene composure after the murder and showed his legal skill and self-confidence in the way in which he argued his case in English, a language he supposedly did not know well. Ashis Nandy says that it was as if the assassination gave meaning and drive to a life which otherwise was becoming increasingly prosaic. Godse was extremely religious. He read into the *Gita* with his martial background. For him Krishna was speaking to Arjuna about*real battles* and not allegorical battles fought in the inner self. Tilak's ethics of intrinsic goodness of violence had once again come back to life. It was once again seen as a sacred duty of the patriots of the Hindu *rashtra*.

Gandhi was denounced by Hindutva ideologues for preaching and practising the doctrine of *ahimsa* (non-violence) in the most 'perverted form'. He was killed by a Hindu for having undermined and betrayed Hindu India. Gopal Godse, brother of Nathuram Godse says: 'Our motive was not to achieve control of the government; ... we were simply trying to rid the nation of someone who had done and was doing great harm to it. He had consistently insulted the Hindu nation and had weakened it by his doctrine of *ahimsa*". Patrick Nair reports that at Nagpur the RSS have built a shrine in honour of Godse. While visiting Nagpur in the 1980s he wandered into the RSS complex and found a shrine dedicated to Nathuram Godse. It had a plaque with the message that one day when the Hindu nationalists come to power a far more fitting memorial would be erected. Prior to 30 January 1948, there had been five known unsuccessful attempts to kill Gandhi, all of them except one in Maharashtra – the land of Tilak. The first was in Poona in June 1934 when Gandhi was engaged in an anti-untouchability campaign there. The second, in July 1944, at Panchgani where Nathuram Godse, dressed in a Nehru shirt, pyjama and jacket, rushed towards Gandhi brandishing a dagger in his hand and shouting anti-Gandhi slogans. But he was overpowered by the people around Gandhi. The third, in September 1944, at Sevagram which also involved Godse along with some others. The fourth, in June 1946, near Poona when some unknown persons tried to derail the train in which Gandhi was travelling. The fifth, on 20 January 1948 in New Delhi which involved a bomb attack.

The unprecedented growth of the RSS and its affiliates and the upsurge of militancy among the Hindus should be seen as one of the effects of the re-reading of Tilak's interpretation of the *Gita*. Following Tilak's example many Hindutva ideologues and organisations are now giving new interpretations not only to the *Gita* but also to other sacred books of the Hindus like, the *Ramayana* and *Mahabharata* and even *Puranas* in order to rationalise violence as a means to promote Hindu cultural nationalism. Referring to *Mahabharata* – of which the *Gita* forms a part – Rajmohan Gandhi says that the epic is a story of unending revenge and violence.

In his own time Tilak became the guru of V.D.Savarkar (1883-1966), especially in his extreme ideology of nationalism. It was Tilak who recommended the case of Savarkar for a scholarship to go to

London for studies. In London Savarkar was busy with production of bombs, eventually sending a manual on this subject back to Tilak, publication of revolutionary pamphlets, books, etc. The founder of the RSS, Keshav Baliram Hedgewar (1889-1940) also came under the influence of Tilak. Another prominent RSS leader who was influenced by Tilak was Balkrishna Shivaram Moonje (1872-1948) the founder of the Bhonsle Military School in Nasik. Madhav Kashinath Damley founder of *Lokhandi Morcha* or *Iron Front*, a Fascist movement, was also a follower of Tilak. Tilak's thoughts have influenced the Hindu Mahasabha, the Jan Sangh and the RSS. The RSS subscribe to Tilak's understanding of *karma-yoga* and the *swayamsevaks* are advised to read the *Gita* regularly. Krishna Kumar writing about the revival of Hindu nationalism in India says: "the RSS was a blossom of the vigorous seed of revivalist nationalism that Tilak had sown". Almost all those convicted in the trial of Gandhi murder case had a connection, past or present with either the Hindu Mahasabha or the RSS and they were believers in violence.

Many Hindutva ideologues make strenuous effort to popularise the view that the Hindu gods and goddesses are 'weapon wielding deities'. In 1966 N.N.Banerjee, president of the Hindu Mahasabha, on the occasion of the golden jubilee of the organisation told the Hindus that all their deities, such as, Siva, Vishnu, Durga, Kali, Kartikeya, Shri Ramachandra, Shri Krishna are warriors and they carry weapons. Hence Hindus need to realise their significance and should become their dynamic worshippers. Aurobindo reminds us that in the *Mahabharata*, Krishna says that God created battle and armour, the sword, the bow and the dagger.

Describing Goddess Kali, V.S.Naipaul says: "Kali, 'the black one', the coal-black aboriginal goddess, surviving in Hinduism as the emblem of female destructiveness, garlanded with human skulls, tongue forever out for fresh blood, eternally sacrificed to but insatiable". Ashis Nandy states that Kali is the new symbol of a treacherous cosmic mother, eager to betray and prone to aggression, fierce, violent, associated with robbers, thieves, thugs, prostitutes, and in some of her incarnations she was associated with certain dangerous diseases. B.Walker says that Kali holds in two of her hands a sword and a dagger and in the other two are severed heads dripping with blood. Her long tongue hangs out of her mouth and blood trickles down her chin and neck as she gorges herself at her cannibal feasts. In one hideous image a headless Kali holds her own severed head, while the mouth greedily drinks the blood spurting from her neck.

Rama of *Ramayana* is depicted as wielding a bow and arrow. In fact, the symbol of the Shiv Sena is Ram's bow and arrow. He is also projected as the national hero of the Hindu nation. Hanuman is the monkey-god who served Rama with steadfast devotion. But he is also a symbol of irrational destruction. He went to Lanka in search of Sita. Before he left he destroyed everything in sight, razing houses and uprooting trees as though they were grass until he was captured by Indrajit, son of Ravana. In a bid to humiliate Hanuman and send him back to Ram, an oil-soaked cloth was tied to his tail and set alight.

But Hanuman, charged through the city and the surrounding countryside causing untold havoc and burning all the crops with his fiery tail. Today Hanuman is the model for the Bajrang Dal activists – the Indian version of the Nazi Stormtroopers (SA, *Sturmabteilung* 'storming department'). Durga Vahini cadets emulate the Goddess Durga, the demon-killing protective mother, who is actually supposed to be the goddess Kali. Many Hindutva ideologues now speak of militant Hinduism as the 'Third Eye' of the Hindu. M.M.Ahluwalia maintains that the Hindu revolutionaries were influenced by the European revolutionaries on the one hand and the militancy of Hindu gods and goddesses and historical heroes on the other. Many Bengali secret societies were inspired by Tilak's interpretation of the *Gita.*

The members of the *Anushilan Samiti* ('disciplinary organisation') took an oath of allegiance to the organisation before an image of Goddess Kali with the *Bhagavadgita* in one hand and a revolver in the other. Aurobindo envisaged *karma yoga* as a means of legitimising violence as a form of sacrifice. He believed in an aggressive Hinduism. According to him open attack, unsparing criticism, the severest satire, the most wounding irony, are all methods perfectly justifiable and indispensable in politics. In 1951 N.C.Chatterjee as president of the Hindu Mahasabha said: "The greatest task of the Mahasabha is to create Hindu character on the basis of the Geetha (sic)". In 1960, V.G.Deshpande in his presidential address of the 45th Annual Session of the All India Hindu Mahasabha spoke of the need to resort to guerrilla and mountain warfare. The *karma yoga* expounded in the *Gita* is practised by the RSS *pracharaks* ('preachers') which is described as a matter of inner sacrifice. They maintain that action, even when violent, can constitute a means of renunciation when it is undertaken without regard to personal advantage and in the service of Hindu nation (*rashtra*) and Hindu *dharma*.

Many Nazis of Germany took inspiration from the *Gita*. For example, Heinrich Himmler (1900-1945), the chief of Hitler's security service (SS, *Schutzstaffel = security guard*) constantly carried with him this sacred book, cited from it, compared Hitler to Lord Krishna and wanted his SS troop to be like the Kshatriya caste of India which saw war as part of their spirituality. Savitri Devi (1905-1982) a staunch Nazi (popularly known as 'Hitler's Priestess') was the first woman writer who regarded Adolf Hitler as a divine incarnation equal of Ram and Krishna in the *Gita*. She justified the elimination of millions of Jews in Nazi Germany by quoting from the *Gita*. Devi also considered the *Schutzstaffel* of Hitler as the incarnation of the Indo-Aryan Kshatriya caste. According to Victor and Victoria Trimondi, the *Gita* spiritualises cruelty (*skralisierung der Grausamkeit*). All imaginable forms of cruelty were practised in the fratricidal war described in the *Gita*. In addition, Hitler envisaged cruelty as a virtue of the new generation of Nazi youth.

Writing in the 1960s K.M.Panikkar said that the *Gita* has become the scripture of the new age, the main foundation on which its ethic, its social doctrines and even its political action depends. The Rama myth is a help to rationalise the aggressiveness and violence of the Shiv Sena, VHP, BJP, RSS, Bajrang Dal and the Sangh Parivar as a whole. Rama is the new icon of the anti-Muslim movement in India as was Shivaji in Tilak's time. *Mahabharata* is seen as a scripture of war. The televising of *Ramayana* (1987-1989 in 91 weekly episodes) and *Mahabharata* (1988-1990 in 94 episodes) helped the Hindu masses to imbibe the spirit of violence from their favourite sacred books, gods and goddesses. Today, the sacred books of Hinduism – which are meant to guide the everyday religious code of the Hindus – are often used to extol violence for a so-called 'greater cause'. The saffronised NCERT school textbook of Social Sciences for Class IX extols revolutionaries like Tilak, Aurobindo, V.D.Savarkar, G.D. Savarkar, Swami Saradhananda, Sister Nivedita, and militant organisations like *Anushilan Samiti* (Bengal), *Yugantar* Party (Bengal, led by Barindra Ghose brother of Aurobindo Ghose), *Abhinav Bharat* (in Maharashtra, led by Savarkar brothers), Baroda Secret Society (Maharashtra), etc.

In 1991 the BJP campaigned vigorously for the extension of a Sunday morning television serial depicting the life of the famous Indian political philosopher, Chanakya or Kautilya (the word 'Kautilya' means 'crookedness and treachery'), the reputed author of *Arthasastra*, a hand book of totalitarian, ruthless and cynical stagecraft characterised by depravity in standards of morality. The serial portrayed Chanakya's struggle to assist Chandra Gupta Maurya (320-297 B.C) in ancient India in a way to suggest its similarities to the struggle waged by the BJP then to seize political power in New Delhi. But those who are familiar with the functioning of the BJP knows that much of its ethics is 'chanakyan' where 'end justifies the means'. Its 'India Shining', 'Feel Good', 'Super Power India' slogans were founded on chanakyan cut-throat ethics of lies, crookedness and ruthlessness with the desire to win 300 seats in the Indian parliament during the general elections of 2004 – a dubious heritage from Tilak's ethics of expediency.

But Tilak interpreted it in the interest of his political expediency and twisted its message to justify violence, extremism and militancy. Today, some Hindutva ideologues consider him as the person who freed the Indian National Congress from the so-called scourge of moderation. Tilak selectively cited from the *Gita* in order to justify his ethical stand and he believed in the intrinsic goodness of violence. This might be the reason why he said that politics is a game of worldly people and not of *sadhus*.

Tilak's experiment of combining religion and politics became a model for the Hindutva ideologues of contemporary India. Communal violence in India today is frequently and almost ubiquitously justified by using Hindu scriptures, especially the *Gita*, *Ramayana* and

Mahabharta. Many interpret them literally, and indulge in the most eccentric forms violence against their enemies without qualms of conscience.

Arvind Sharma remarks that it was more than a mere curiosity that both Mahatma Gandhi and his assassin Nathuram Godse swore by the *Bhagavadgita* – one by its figurative interpretation and the other by its literal. S.C. Sen Gupta observes that the *Gita* is patently a call to arms, an exposition of the doctrine of violence when it becomes a duty. B.R. Ambedkar, criticising Hinduism and its the tendency towards violence, observes that the *Gita* is about the justification of war; Krishna offers a philosophical defence of war and killing in war.

During the *rath yatra* of L.K.Advani in 1990, in many places the most common offering was traditional weaponry: arrows, dices, maces, swords, trident and *kripans*. At Jetpur in Gujarat 101 kshatriya youths offered him a bowl containing their blood. No wonder why V.S.Naipaul says: "I think religion is the greatest curse of mankind. It has killed more people, destroyed more property, than any other thing".

6

Tilak's Philosophy for the Nation

Lord Macaulay's Indian intellectuals, the leaders of Westernisation in social and political reform, based their programme of social and political action almost entirely on the philosophy of life and action of nineteenth century Europe. They were truly more the products of Western civilization than Indian. Tilak was not satisfied with the Western values and was not ready to reject India's own philosophy of life in order to imitate the philosophy of the British.

For Tilak, there was no reason for India to feel ashamed of her civilization when compared to the west. Just the contrary, India should feel great pride. Indian values were different from but not inferior to western values. Dharma, according to Tilak was the integrative principal, and Swadharma the spiritual and social duty of each individual. Here was the guide to social and political action.

The Westernized intellectuals (mainly social reformers) wanted to change and remake India in an alien faith. But they were wrong. Tilak reminded them, "How can a man be proud of the greatness of his own nation if he feels no pride of his own religion?" It was the Bharadharma that provided an understanding of the moral purposefulness of the universe, which is the necessary basis of a philosophy of life. It provided Tilak and the nationalists like Ghose, Pal, and Lal with a guide to concrete action in personal, social and political matters. From an Indian philosophy of life Tilak and the nationalist leaders began to construct an Indian philosophy of politics that was to become the political theory of the Indian Independence Movement. He became the chief architect of the political philosophy of the Indian independence movement as he was one of the most important leaders of India at that time.

Two Festivals

Perhaps the most effective way in which he reached the people was through the employment of national festivals. He was instrumental in popularizing two great festivals, one to Ganapati, the Hindu deity of learning and propitiousness, and a festival to revive the memory of glory of Shivaji, the liberator of Maharashtra, and the restorer of Swaraj through his battle with the Mughal Empire. He especially emphasised the dynamic spirit of Shivaji. He believed it was the spirit which actuated Shivaji in his doings that is held forth as the proper idea to be kept constantly in view of the rising generation. To keep this spirit constant, Tilak worked ceaselessly to reach the people and to educate them through the festivals. He carried his doctrine throughout Maharashtra and waged his battle. Education through religion and history, through the association in the popular mind with gods and heroes, through recreating an appreciation of the heritage of the past as a guide to the future. This was the way he educated the people.

First Sedition Case (1897)

Tilak was aggressive and writing very strongly through the editorials of Kesari against the British bureaucracy.

The British bureaucracy and the Anglo-Indian press realised that Tilak was an emerging leader of the people and of a new spirit in India. Those who lacked foresight began to fear him.

In the tense atmosphere of famine and a plague—racked Pune, a young man, Damodar Chaphekar assassinated Rand. Rand was the British official in charge of the plague. Those who feared Rand, were quick to blame Tilak for the death, and hinted at his complicity in a conspiracy for political assassination. Tilak was, of course, innocent of any knowledge of or collaboration in this crime. He had publically disagreed with Rand for his unsympathetic behaviour towards the plague stricken people. Tilak had condemned the inhuman aspects of the British anti-plague campaign, but he had never contemplated or encouraged the assassination of the British official in charge. Tilak, nevertheless, was brought to trial in 1897, not as an accessory to assassination, not as being involved in the plot to commit murder, but rather on the charge of 'sedition'.

The court allowed the prosecution to argue that he had written seditious matter and his criminal sedition constituted, in effect, 'dissatisfaction' with the British Raj. It was brought to the notice of the court that Tilak was not positively "affectionate for" British officialdom. This was one of the most unusual interpretations of 'sedition and disaffection' in the annals of British justice. Nevertheless Tilak was convicted and sentenced to two years' imprisonment. The British had miscalculated both the effect of this sentence on Tilak and on public opinion.

N.C. Kelkar observes, "His arrest and prosecution in 1897 was a sensation that nearly pulled the mind of the country by its roots, as political prosecutions were then extremely rare, and Tilak was, in himself a man big enough to mark an epoch by his personal misfortune."

But this was not Tilak's last imprisonment. The British Indian Government endeavoured to convict him of perjury in connection with the well-known Tai Maharaj case in 1904. They did not succeed as he was acquitted by the High Court. In 1908, he was sentenced to six years' imprisonment, again for sedition; but in 1916, he was acquitted of a similar charge. For two decades he was persecuted by the British Indian Government because they saw in him the greatest challenge to their rule over the Indian empire.

The seditation case in 1897 roused sympathy not only in Maharashtra but also in Bengal. In Bengal, Shishir Kumar Motilal Ghosh and Surendranath Bannerjee started raising funds for the defense of Tilak. The court found Tilak guilty but Tilak's prestige rose very high in the minds of the people. Max Mueller and Indian leaders submitted a memorial to the government for the early release of Tilak. The government also soon realised the mistake and released Tilak.

Tilak emerged from prison in 1899 (first sedition) after serving eighteen months of his sentence. Now he became a national hero. He got following outside Maharashtra. He became the first all-India national leader. He had been persecuted for his political opinions. He was now the acknowledged political leader of the nation and the nation was prepared to heed his opinions. He had begun as an awakener of the people and as a critic of bureaucratic abuses. He emerged from prison with the responsibility of leading the Nationalist cause to political self-determination (Swatantrya). He was acclaimed the Lokmanya, the honoured and respected of the people.

Tilak's knowledge and love of the great classical Indian values had prepared him with a personal philosophy and a frame of reference for his battles with social reformism and with the spirit of orthodoxy. It also provided him with the foundation of his emerging political philosophy. He had fought against injustice, he had argued against the placating policies of the moderates. Now he began to put forward a positive political programme centred around the concept of Swaraj, self-rule for India. He realised that the self-rule must precede the meaningful social reform.

National self-rule, he believed, was the only enduring basis for national unity and national self-respect. He reminded people that Shivaji had recreated Swaraj as a necessary foundation of social and political freedom, progress and morality. He, therefore, declared, which in course of time became a famous slogan, that "swaraj is my birth right and I shall have it".

A CRITICAL EVALUATION OF TILAK'S PHILOSOPHY

Tilak created a revolution in the world of ethics with his *Gitarahasya*. It had far reaching consequences in the field of religion, politics, relationship with religious minorities and national struggle for independence. Below we take a critical look at his ethical views and its impact on the Hindutva ideology which is in vogue.

K.M.Panikkar observes that it is Tilak's *Gitarahasya* which marked the change in Indian political scenario. He showed for the first time that the message of the *Gita* was not renunciation as others had thought before, but it was essentially a scripture preaching a doctrine of social activism where action for human good without personal attachment is preached as the first imperative.

Subjective Interpretation of the *Gita*

Richard Charles Zaehner says that in interpreting the *Gita*, as in interpreting any sacred text, the danger is that the interpreter will quote all that is grist to his mill while failing to draw attention to what embarrasses him in other parts of the text.

Tilak introduced a new trend in the reading of scriptures with his *Gitarahasya*, namely, that of giving a subjective interpretation to the Hindu scriptures in order to give foundation for his concept of violence as higher duty. It is said that 'what one ought to do' is the problem of morality. The *Gita* says that what ought to be done is one's caste duty. If we follow Tilak's *Gitarahasya* the caste duty consists in action which may involve also violence, and it is fully justified. This is of course abuse of caste power.

The traditional Hindu texts like the *Gita* took on unprecedented importance with Tilak's *Gitarahasya*. The *Gita* became for the Hindu reformers a kind of counter Bible. Consequently many translations of the *Gita* were sponsored throughout the subcontinent in various languages. Until the advent of Tilak, the interpretations given to the *Gita* never really advocated violence. Many of the great Hindu reformers felt compelled to compose their own 'reading' or commentary of it. Thus not only do we hear from the more spiritual reformers such as, Swami Vivekananda (1863-1902), Sarveppalli Radhakrishnan (1888-1975) or Vinoba Bhave (1895-1994) but also men of action like Gandhi. But their concept of *karma yoga* differed from Tilak's.

The great commentators of the *Gita* preferred non-violence than violence. Some saw in the *Gita* action for social reform, others action for political independence, and some others saw in it a call to take up arms.

For the most part, the overwhelming majority of commentators read the *Gita* non-violently, as a spiritual or moral allegory and the desire to avoid violence was ever present. Many made allegorical readings of the battle between the Pandavas and the Kauravas. Gandhi saw the *Mahabharata* itself as a 'great anti-war epic' and Krishna's conversation with Arjuna as imaginary. This interpretation became the dominant reading of the *Gita* during the twentieth century. But with Tilak it was different.

In his own time Gandhi had rejected the views of Tilak. He said: "I do not find myself in agreement with everything he [Tilak] says"; "What we need to consider is whether Indians should accept the views of Mr.Tilak and his party. We submit, after great deliberation, that Mr.Tilak's views should be rejected".

K.M.Panikkar tells us that the British government was not unaware of the dynamite that the *Gita* contained, for long before Tilak's *Gitarahasya* had been published, he had been preaching its message. The authorities even considered seriously the question of proscribing the *Gita*; but a holy book which the Hindu masses use as daily prayer and which has been translated into every Indian language could not be proscribed as a seditious volume.

Divine Sanction to Violence

Tilak's interpretation of the *Gita* was an attempt to find justification for violence and militancy in the Hindu scriptures. An action may involve violence. But when that action is seen as a duty, violence becomes unavoidable and necessary. Tilak goes a step further and gives it a divine sanction. He presents Krishna as the new law-giver. This makes his ethics even more dangerous and diabolic. Thus violence becomes a religious activity, an obligation (*dharma*) for all Hindus and salvation is to be achieved through it. This makes us raise two pertinent questions: can a subjective interpretation of sacred scripture to rationalise violence be justified? Can such an interpretation be declared as divinely sanctioned? As we have seen above, according to Tilak, both are possible.

Tilak's ethics has been a great attraction for many Hindutva ideologues and organisations of modern and contemporary India.

Hindu sacred scriptures like the *Bhagavadgita*, *Ramayana* and *Mahabharata* and even some *Puranas* are liberally interpreted in order to justify militancy, violence and extremism aganist both real and imaginary enemies in many parts of India. Ashis Nandy is correct to some extent when he says that South Asian gods and goddesses, like their Hellenistic counterparts, can sometimes be found on the wrong side of morality and law.

Many modern and contemporary Hindutva ideologues were inspired by Tilak's interpretation of the *Gita*. For example, M.S.Golwalkar, who was the leader of the RSS from 1940 to 1973 said: "Our Philosophy teaches us to fight with all our strength, [...] Sri Krishna commands Arjuna to fight, [...] and in a spirit of doing one's duty unwaveringly". Aurobindo said: "It is an error to think that the heights of religion are above the struggles of this world. The recurrent cry of Sri Krishna to Arjuna insists on the struggle: 'Fight and overthrow thy opponents'".

Pravin Togadia, a prominent leader of the VHP says: "during the Mahabharata, did God ask Arjuna not to fight, did God talk to Arjun about *Ahimsa*? What had Krishna Bhagawan said? Fight. [....] He told Arjuna to kill Karna. This is what Kyshtriya [sic] blood is made up of. Karna was killed. Did anyone tell Krishna that he had followed a path of *adharma*?".

There is nothing as dangerous as giving divine sanction to violence. It easily convinces the naive and the ignorant to indulge in violence as there is merit attached to it. It makes the criminals to commit violence with religious fervour.

Many instances of communal violence in India are violence justified by religion. In 1992 those who died during the *kar seva* in order to demolish the Babri mosque are considered as martyrs. On 6 December 1992 at Ayodhya in the midst of the hysterical cries of the *karsevaks, Jai siya Ram* the Babri mosque was razed to the ground. The attack on a century-old Christian Girl's school at Rajkot on 20 June 1998 was carried out amidst shouting slogans of *Jai Shri Ram*. The same slogan was heard when the Australian missionary Graham Staines and his two sons were burned alive in Orissa in 1999. When the Muslims women were being gang raped at Godhra in Gujarat in early 2002 the rapists shouted *har har Mahadev*.

Religious sanction to violence helps militants and extremists to plan to the finest details the execution of their misdeeds. Thus acts of violence become a sort of sacred ritual, the criminals assume the role of high priests and what is promised to the accomplices in the crime is merit.

Justification of Hindu Militancy

Tilak represented a militant version of Hinduism. He argues that Hinduism is a warrior-religion with a warrior-morality. Lord Krishna did not send Arjuna to the woods as a mendicant or make a *sanyasin* out of him, filling his mind with apathy. He did not place in his hands cymbals or drum or harp but bow and arrows. His advice to Arjuna was to fight: "therefore, O Arjuna, fight"; "therefore, determine to fight and rise"; 'therefore, think of me [Krishna] and fight"; "the doer and the causer of everything is I myself [Krishna], and you [Arjuna] are only the tool; and therefore, fight and conquer your enemies". Tilak reminds us that Arjuna did really fight, and in the course of the fight he actually killed Bhisma, Karna, Jayadratha, and others as occasion arose. In other words, according to Tilak, in modern terms, a true patriot is one who holds the *Gita* on the one hand and pistol on the other.

Gandhi once remarked that Tilak seems to have said that in our language we have no word corresponding to conscience. Therefore, he rejected the idea of conscience. Gandhi was of the opinion that Tilak missed the inner meaning of the *Gita* when he used it to justify violence. He says: "But I have often felt that he [Tilak] has not understood the age-old spirit of India, has not understood her soul", which according to Gandhi, is non-violence (*ahimsa*).

During the trial of Tilak the judge said the following about him in the sentence he delivered: "It seems to me that it must be a diseased mind, a most perverted mind, that could say that the articles which you have written are legitimate weapons in political agitation. They are seething with sedition; they breathe violence; they speak of murder with approval, and the cowardly and atrocious act of committing murder with bombs not only seems to meet with your approval, but you hail that advent of the bomb in India as if something had come to India for good".

Violence is energy and talents wasted. The Judge added: "you [Tilak] are a man of undoubted talents and great power and influence. Those talents and influence if used for the good of your country would have been instrumental in brining about a great deal of happiness for those very people whose cause you expose".

Thus, as K.M.Panikkar observes, the terrorists and other political groups which worked for revolution believed frankly in violence and elevated it to a creed, and with the beginning of the twentieth century a new type of nationalism which believed in revolutionary methods emerged. The leaders of this new movement were Tilak in Western India and Aurobindo Ghose in Bengal.

7

Tilak and Home Rule Movement

HOME RULE FLAG

The All India Home Rule League was a national political organization founded in 1916 to lead the national demand for self-government, termed *Home Rule*, and to obtain the status of a Dominion within the British Empire as enjoyed by Australia, Canada, South Africa, New Zealand and Newfoundland at the time.

In Context of World War I

Most Indians and Indian political leaders had been divided in their response to World War I and the Indian soldiers fighting on behalf of the British Empire against Germany, the Austro-Hungarian Empire and the Ottoman Empire. The latter's involvement irked India's Muslims, who saw the Sultan as the Caliph of Islam. Many Indian revolutionaries opposed the war, while moderates and liberals backed the war. The issue divided India's political classes and left the increasing demand for self-government going nowhere.

FOUNDING

Between 1916 and 1918, when the war was closing, prominent Indians like Muhammad Ali Jinnah, Bal Gangadhar Tilak and the leader of the Theosophical Society, Annie Besant decided to organize a national alliance of leagues across India, specifically to demand *Home Rule*, or self-government within the British Empire for all of India. Tilak founded the first League in the city of Pune, Maharashtra. Muhammad Ali Jinnah headed up the League's Bombay Branch. With its national headquarters in Delhi, the main cities of activity were Bombay, Calcutta and Madras.

The move created considerable excitement at the time, and attracted many members of the Indian National Congress and the All India Muslim League, who had been allied since the 1916 Lucknow Pact. The leaders of the League gave fiery speeches, and petitions with hundreds of thousands of Indians as signatories were submitted to British authorities.

Unification of moderates and radicals as well as unity between Muslim League and Indian National Congress was a remarkable achievement of Mrs Annie Besant. Later when government arrested Annie Besant the movement actually spread out and made its impact in interior villages of India. League spread the political awareness in new areas like Sindh, Punjab, Gujarat, United Provinces, Bihar, Orissa as well as Madras and all stood up for an active political movement, qasdas sdl, las, md asda.

FORMATION OF INDIAN NATIONAL CONGRESS

Allen Octavian Hume at last shaped the Indian National Congress. The First meeting was in December 1885 in Bombay. Womesh Chandra Banerjee turned into the primary president of Indian National Congress. It met each year in December in various parts of the nation. In the early years, the congress utilized just Petition, Prayer and Protest to attempt to get their requirements met. In 1891 Indian plant Act was passed and in 1892 Indian Councils Act was changed to incorporate new arrangements for administrating India. Bubonic Plague in Bombay, 1896-1914 and Indian Famine 1897-1901:

> *The epidemic spread from Bombay City, western and northern India, was hardest hit. Around 200,000 people died of plague in Bombay alone. Between October 1896 and February 1897, nearly half of Bombay's estimated 850,000 populations left the city resulting in great loss to commerce and industrial*

life and helped the disease to spread in countryside and other parts of India. Along with plague many parts of India were devastated by famine during 1897-1901 that killed around 2 million people.

FIRST PARTITION OF BENGAL

Following the 'divide and rule' policy Bengal was divided by the British, on October 16, 1905, into Hindu and Muslim areas. By doing this British had hoped to increase tensions between the Hindus and the Muslims. Lord Curzon was the British governor general at this time. The following excerpts from Curzon's letter of 2nd February 1905 to St. John Brodrick, Secretary of State for India, give an idea of his aims in partitioning Bengal.

"CALCUTTA is the center from which the Congress Party is manipulated throughout the whole of Bengal, and indeed the whole of India. Its best wire pullers and its most frothy orators all reside here. The perfection of their machinery, and the tyranny which it enables them to exercise are truly remarkable. They dominate public opinion in Calcutta; they affect the High Court; they frighten the local Government, and they are sometimes not without serious influence on the Government of India. The whole of their activity is directed to creating an agency so powerful that they may one day be able to force a weak government to give them what they desire. Any measure in consequence that would divide the Bengali-speaking population; that would permit independent centres of activity and influence to grow up; that would dethrone Calcutta from its place as the centre of successful intrigue, or that would weaken the influence of the lawyer class, who have the entire organization in their hands, is intensely and hotly resented by them. The outcry will be loud and very fierce, but as a native gentleman said to me – 'my countrymen always howl until a thing is settled; then they accept it'."

Protest meetings against the partition were organized in all parts of the country on and after 16 October 1905. Partition of Bengal also saw a strong polarization in Indian National Congress between 'moderates' and 'hardliners'. Moderates such as Gopal Krishan Gokhale believed in making "loyal" representations to the government for small reforms, while hardliners like Lokmanya Bal Gangadhar Tilak complete freedom or 'purna swarajya'.

Tilak announced his slogan "Swaraj is my birthright and I shall have it" in his newspaper and became the speaker for the new group of nationalists. The primary leaders of the nationalist movement were Lala Lajpat Rai (1865-1928) from Punjab, Lokmanya Bal Gangadhar Tilak (1856-1920) from Maharashtra and Bipin Chandra Pal from Bengal. Together, they were called Lal-Bal-Pal. Ajit Singh in Punjab and Chidambaram Pillay in Tamil Nadu were other important leaders of the Nationalistic Movement.

In 1906, Tilak set forth a programme of passive resistance, known as the Tenets of the New Party, that he hoped would destroy the hypnotic influence of British rule and prepare the people for sacrifice in order to gain independence. Mahatma Gandhi later adopted these forms of political action initiated by Tilak-the boycotting of goods and passive resistance-in his programme of non-cooperation with the British.

The Nationalistic movement adopted the slogan of "Swadeshi and Swaraj". Swadeshi means our country and promoted the use of Indian products and the boycott of foreign goods. Swaraj means self-government.

Tilak aimed at Swarajya (Independence), not piecemeal reforms, and attempted to persuade the Congress to adopt his purna swarajya programme. On this issue, he clashed with the moderates at the Surat session of the Congress in 1907. Taking advantage of the split in the nationalist forces, the government again prosecuted Tilak on a charge of sedition and inciting terrorism and deported him to Mandalay, Burma (Myanmar), to serve a sentence of six years' imprisonment.

FORMATION OF MUSLIM LEAGUE (1906)

Huge numbers of the Indian Muslims were taken in by British divisive approach of 'partition and run the show'. Despite the fact that

Muslims had a reasonable representation in Congress some of them needed a different stage for Indian Muslims. In 1906 Muslim League was shaped to speak to Indian Muslims.

By the segment of Bengal in 1905 British effectively sowed the seeds of division amongst Hindus and Muslims that lead at last to the segment of India in 1947. Apparitions of the British 'gap and run' approach, keep on haunting free India and Pakistan in present times with proceeding with strains and fringe question.

EARLY REVOLUTIONARY MOVEMENT

Partition of Bengal created a massive outburst of public anger against British rule. Intellectual people as well as common man took part in mass agitation. Poet Rabindranath Tagore actively supported the movement. Bankim Chandra Chatterjee's '*Bande Matram*' was taken up as the soul-stirring slogan. Several groups of revolutionaries started operating in Bengal. Aurobindo Ghosh (later known as Sri Aurobindo), Rasbihari Bose and Jatindranath Mukherjee (Bagha Jatin) were some of the important leaders of these revolutionary groups.

ALIPORE BOMB CASE

On 30th April, 1908 in Muzzafarpur Bihar, Khudiram Bose and Prafulla Chaki tried to kill the Chief Presidency Magistrate Kingsford who was notorious for passing out stiff sentences against the nationalist activists Kingsford escaped the bomb attack which unfortunately killed two innocent British ladies died in the bomb attack. Following a massive manhunt, Khudiram was arrested on 1st May 1908; Prafulla evaded arrest by shooting himself. On 11th August 1908, eighteen-year-old Khudiram Bose was hanged and became a martyr. Aurobindo Ghosh was arrested on charges of masterminding the attacks on Kingsford but a young lawyer Chittaranjan Das ably defended him. Aurobindo later left politics and became a Yogi and philosopher and became famous as Maharishi Aurobindo or Sri Aurobindo. A Durbar was held in Delhi on December 12, 1911, to celebrate the visit of King George V. King was welcomed with great pomp and show and given numerous priceless gifts. In 1911 British government under pressure from increasing agitations in Bengal and other parts of India modified the 'partition of Bengal' to make again a united Presidency of Bengal.

HARDINGE BOMB CASE

British shifted the imperial capital from Calcutta to Delhi in 1912. On December 23, 1912 to mark the entry of the Governor-general of India into the new Capital, an imperial procession was taken out in Delhi, with Lord Hardinge seated on a caparisoned elephant. As the procession was passed through Chandni Chowk, a bomb was thrown on the elephant, killing the *mahawat*. Lord Hardinge escaped with injuries. Many persons including Master Amir Chand, a school teacher of Delhi, Bhai Balmukand, Master Awadh Behari, Basant Kumar Biswas, Ganeshilal Khasta, Vishnu Ganesh Pingley, Charan Das, Balraj, Lachhmi Narain Sharma and Lala Hanwant Sahey, and many others were arrested. L.N Sharma and G. Khasta were taken to Varanasi and sentenced to life imprisonment. V.G Pingley was taken to Lahore and was hanged. Master Amir Chand, Bhai Balmukand and Master Awadh Behari were executed on May 8, 1915 in Delhi Jail and Basant Kumar Biswas was executed the next day on May 9, 1915 in Ambala Central Jail.

Ras Bihari Bose, who masterminded the Chandni Chowk incident, escaped to Japan and continued the struggle against British rule from abroad. He was the President of Indian Independence League and head of the first Indian National Army (INA) founded by General Mohan Singh.

In 1914 Britain became engaged in World War I. Shortly after declaration of war, two infantry divisions and a cavalry brigade of the Indian Army were sent to Europe. In all 140,000 men served on the Western Front, 90,000 in the Indian Corps and 50,000 in the Labour Companies. Indian troops also played important role in operations in Mesopotamia, Palestine, and Gallipoli. They also served in the West and East African campaigns and in China.

On 16 June 1914, Bal Gangadhar Tilak was released after serving a prison sentence of 6 years, most of which he had spent in Mandalay in Burma. In 1915-1916, under the leadership of Tilak, Annie Besant and Subramaniya Iyer, the Home Rule League was started. January 9, 1915, saw the beginning of a new phase in India's struggle for independence with arrival of Mohandas Karamchand Gandhi to Bombay from South Africa. Two major events took place at the Lucknow session of the Indian Nation Congress in 1916. First, the moderate and hardliner groups were united. Second, the Muslim League put aside old differences and joined hands with the Indian National Congress. Responding to Gandhi's call for helping British in World War I, a large number of Indians joined British Indian Army during 1916-1917. By the end of the World War I in 1918, the numerical strength of Indians in British Indian Army had increased to nearly 600,000.

First Stirrings of Nationalism

On Tuesday, June 22, 1897, the British in India were engaged in celebrating the Diamond Jubilee of the Queen-Empress Victoria. They did so with military parades, dances and champagne dinners. At Poona, the summer seat of the Governor of Bombay, the festivities were particularly glittering. That night there was a dinner-party at Government House. As the guests left in their carriages they were startled by the sound of firing. A woman's screams brought the guests and guards to two carriages in which one man, Walter Rand lay dying and another, Charles Ayrest, was dead. Political assassination had emerged as a weapon against the British Raj.

The authorities were caught off balance, but not for long. Surprise was replaced by angry panic. Was the murder of Englishmen an signal for a popular uprising? The Indians certainly had many reasons to revolt. A serious famine in Western India followed by the appearance for the first time in India of bubonic plague. Doctors knew neither the cause of, nor the cure for this terrifying scourge. In Bombay alone, 20,000 died, and by 1897 the disease had spread to the countryside. In Poona, the Chief Plague Officer, Mr. Rand, whose reputation as a stern disciplinarian had preceded him, had adopted brutal methods to prevent the spread of infection. British troops had been called in to destroy property believed contaminated. Men, women and children, from allegedly infected areas had been segregated in special plague camps. The troops were not gentle. While searching houses for suspected victims, they damaged religious shrines, looted, and often sent to camps people who were in fact free from the plague.

To the inhabitants of Poona, Mr. Rand's men appeared to be carry on a reign of terror. The native-language press demanded retaliation. Everyone has the right of self defence. According to certain Hindu sects, no blame was attached even to killing if it were disinterested and a group of young men had therefore established a "society for removing obstacles to the Hindu religion" and murdered Mr. Rand and his assistant.

The authorities moved a large force of police into Poona. Secret agents moved among the people, but they could not find the assassins or any clue *t* their identity. A collective fine on the city produced no more than money. But the failure of the police resulted in calls for strong action in the English-language newspapers. Indian nationalism seemed about to embrace violent revolution-a radical and frightening move away from the quiet nationalism that had been the pattern over the previous 30 years.

Indian nationalism was a child of the Raj-at first uncritical and only gradually becoming rebellious. The effects of English education in 19th Century India had been to produce a middle-class identifying itself in many ways with the alien rulers, speaking their language, cherishing their political philosophy, and hoping that the promises so frequently made to them that one day they would be accepted as partners would be fulfilled. As the second half of the 19th Century moved to its close, that fulfilment seemed as far away as ever. The reluctance of the government to share its powers with educated Indians and the unquestioning belief by the British in their racial superiority pushed the middle-classes into action.

At the turn of the century, members of Congress had no desire for independence for India, but only for active participation in the government of the country. They were not anti-British. On the contrary, they believed that the British had brought many blessings to India, and that being a part of the British Empire was not only a gift of Providence but good fortune as well.

The man who emerged during this time as leader of Congress, Gopal Krishna Gokhale, typified these middle-class Indians. He had many British friends and had visited England many times. He believed that the inequalities and inadequacies of Hindu society were the only reason for India's political subordination to their foreign rulers. A cautious rather sickly man, he wanted India to progress gradually in partnership with "the genius of the British people."

But there were others who did not share the faith and hope - and the innocence-of these fully Westernised Indians. Most of them were western educated also, but for them western education had brought unease-and unemployment. In British India there were only a limited number of outlets for the educated. The unemployed found themselves without a place in Westernised society, or in that from which their education cut them off. In fact they began to look upon those Indians who *had* found a place in the world of the British-as government servants, lawyers or businessmen -as just as much their enemies as the British themselves. Had they not become bastard Englishmen? To the educated unemployed, the appeal of religious nationalism offered a refuge, a chance of identity with something greater than themselves.

Given that the first stirrings of religious nationalism occurred in Bengal with the writings of Bankim Chandra Chatterji, there were others too, who claimed to find in the Hindu past a real hope for the future, for an India that was Indian rather than fake British. It was in the province of Bombay that his looking backwards in order to see the shape of the future first took the form of positive political action. The man who gave it that form was Bal Gangadhar Tilak. Western educated, at first cooperative with the moderate English-thinking liberals but soon realised that they represented only a minority, cut away from the people of India. The British, Tilak was convinced, would never give India their freedom, and if they granted some political power it would only be to those who were most in sympathy with their rule. Tilak turned to the organisation of mass action in Bombay province whose inhabitants looked back in admiration to the 17th Century Maratha Empire, which had contained Bombay. There was a recent tradition of Maratha independence.

Tilak quickly assumed leadership of the Hindu masses in Western India. In doing so he was, paradoxically, taking a more orthodox western view of the tools of political change than the Liberal moderates of the Indian National Congress. The history of European democracy in the 19th Century, he said, was the history of revolution not reform. The British did not fear the men of Congress, but they had every reason to fear a popular uprising-and was not assassination a weapon of revolution? This fear turned the British against Tilak and the murders at Poona in 1897.

Yet try as they did, the police could find no connection between Tilak and the murders at Poona. He was therefore charged with sedition. The Governor was reluctant to press such vague charges, but gave in to the clamour of the English press. The trial was a travesty. Two articles by Tilak were subjected to the most perverse interpretation by the presiding judge who defined sedition as "the disaffection" or "want of affection" for British rule. The jury found Tilak guilty by a majority and he was sent to prison for 18 months.

The Politics of Disaster

When natural disasters-famine or plague-hit the sub-continent of India, its British rulers faced up to their responsibilities with varying degrees of vigour and success. The administration's battle against the particularly severe famines at the end of the 19th Century was both energetic and effective. Development projects were set up in affected areas to provide work and wages, the construction of new railways was launched, partly to carry grain to where it was most needed, rent was remitted and a certain amount of free relief was granted. Mercifully, the measures had some effect. The administration's fight against plague, however, was not successful and the Indians were left with an abiding memory of the peremptory and often brutal nature of British paternalism. Well-intentioned action thus intensified nationalism.

The Great Bombay Blunder

The British learned with a vengeance the inadequacies of their short-sighted philanthropy during the Bombay plague of 1896-7.

After a disastrous famine in 1896, bubonic plague broke out in Bombay and spread to Poona. Within a year it had killed 34,000 people. The British adopted drastic measures in their attempt to combat it. Lieutenant Walter Rand a man with a reputation as a strict disciplinarian, was appointed Plague Officer and decided on a draconian policy of isolation. Anyone showing symptoms or suspected of being a contact was shut away in a plague camp. Houses were broken into, hosed down, fumigated and limewashed with no concern for the sensibilities of the inhabitants. The soldiers carried out Rand's orders with a toughness that, on occasion, became brutality. Complaints poured in about women being raped and money stolen.

All sections of the Indian community were outraged. The extremist Bal Gangadhar Tilak, who himself had asked the British for strong measures, headed a deputation to the Governor with suggestions about how the searches could be conducted more humanely. He was politely shown the door. As a direct result of British insensitivity, in 1897, Rand and his deputy were murdered by terrorists. Assassination had for the first time become a political weapon to be used against the British Raj.

Doctor Brighton

In the First World War, when India forgot her quarrel with Britain and helped close the Imperial ranks, 139,000 Indians fought in the mud of the Western front. The British responded generously to such loyalty and to care for the wounded, set up special hospitals along the south coast most notably in Brighton, long known as" Doctor Brighton" for bracing air. George IV's elaborate Indian style Pavilion was aptly fitted out as a hospital, as was the town's 'workhouse,' tactfully renamed the Kitchener Hospital. Every attempt was made to provide comfort for Britain's Eastern soldiers. Different kitchens were opened for different religions. Untouchables were banished to the lawns and the wounded were cared for by orderlies of the same caste. The dead were treated with respect. Muslims were taken for burial to the nearby mosque and Hindus were cremated on a specially built *ghat* near Brighton, and their ashes scattered in the sea.

India Claims Nationhood

The news of Tilak's sentence spread his fame-and his ideas. Young men began to think that their future lay in manipulation of the masses and the use of violence. The moderates had failed them, with their obsequious flattery of alien ideas and their feeble requests for a slice of the cake. Tilak's experience dramatised a conflict of generations. The leaders of Congress were men aware of the century of anarchy that had preceded British rule; but the young felt only the tensions of the time, and their own frustrations. The impatient young men of India, organising themselves into secret societies, reading about European revolutionary terrorism, waited another eight years for some great event that would make them the spearhead of mass protest. The British supplied it with their high-handed decision to divide up the province of Bengal. It had proved too large to be administered as a single unit; now it was to become two separate provinces -West Bengal with a Hindu, and East Bengal and Assam, with a Muslim majority. Here at last was the tinder to spark the flame of Hindu nationalism. Two weapons of protest emerged-the economic boycott of British goods and the terrorists bombs.

The Viceroy, Lord Curzon, who in March 1905 had dismissed the anti-partition agitators as "petty volcanoes" by October, was forced to admit ""the agitation is now being conducted by methods of open terrorism and violence." During 1906, violence spread throughout Bengal. Now secret societies were formed, bomb factories set up. The government assumed special security powers. Leaders were deported without trial, political organisations were declared illegal, many arrests were made and sentences of flogging imposed for many minor crimes. These methods appear to have worked to a certain extent. An attempt by young advocates of violent struggle to capture the leadership of Congress failed. The extremists suffered further setbacks. Their leader Tilak, was once more sentenced in 1908 to eight years in jail. As a sop to the nationalists, 'safe men' *i.e.* Indians with little leverage, were elected to Legislative Councils at vice regal level.

These reforms were the work of Lord Minto, and the cautious Secretary of state for India, John Morley. Both believed that small concessions would encourage those Indians who were loyal to Britain and that India's future would remain firmly in British hands. Morley told Parliament that universal suffrage in India was "a fantastic and ludicrous dream."

The reforms were also well received by Indian Muslims who in 1906-scared at the growing strength of Hindu nationalism and anti-Muslim sentiment, had founded their own political organisation, the Muslim League. They asked for, and were granted separate electorates for Muslims. A dangerous precedent. The commencement of hostilities in Europe in August 1914, produced an outburst of loyal enthusiasm in India, which in the light of subsequent events seems almost incomprehensible. Over a million men volunteered for the armed forces, messages of support came from every level of Indian life, and there were large cash contributions of war loans.

In November 1914, the Under Secretary of State for India emphasised the point in a statement in the House of Commons. "It is clear," he said, "that India claims to be not a mere dependent but a partner in the Empire, and her partnership with us in spirit and on battlefields cannot but alter the angle from which we shall henceforth look at the problems of government of India." By 1915, the extremists had again emerged to voice popular fears and aspirations, their task eased by the death of Gokhale and Sir Pherozshah Mehta, the two most implacable opponents of the extremists in that year.

Indian Muslims too, were no longer so pro-British. The revocation of the partition of Bengal announced at the magnificent Delhi Durbar of 1911, as a sop to Hindu nationalism, had shocked them deeply. They were further alienated from the British by the fact that their spiritual overlord, the Caliph of Turkey, found himself at war with their temporal master the King-Emperor of Britain. Under this pressure, many Muslims, among them the future creator of Pakistan, Muhammad Ali Jinnah urged the League to re-establish the link with the Congress party. In 1916, this occurred, and Britain was once again faced with a united Indian opposition. But the Congress was about to change from a body whose watchword was caution, into a mass rally and the vanguard of militant Hindu nationalism which in turn again split the Muslims from them.

The British managed to dissipate any remaining goodwill by one of the most unimaginative and ill-timed moves they had made during their rule of the Indian subcontinent. At the same time as the Secretary-of-State for India, Edwin Montagu, arrived in India to consult with Indian leaders and the Viceroy, Lord Chelmsford, about impending reforms, a committee under Mr. Justice Rowlatt was sitting to "investigate and report on the nature and extent of the criminal conspiracies connected with the revolutionary movement in India." The Rowlatt Bills effectively guaranteed that Indian nationalists would be suspicious of the proposed reforms.

These reforms-incorporated in the Montagu-Chelmsford Report-which the British hoped would both reward Indian loyalists and stifle unrest, were in fact quite radical, even by the changed standards of the time. The British government not only accepted the principle of self-government for India but was actually ready to prepare for it. But between the announcement of these reforms and their coming into force three years later events took place which were to produce a new national leader-Gandhi-who was to condemn any cooperation with "this satanic government." The Rowlatt Acts were the turning point for the growth of nationalistic fervour in India for, in the atmosphere of tension and indignation which united the political classes and the people as never before, a new leader, Mohandas Karamchand Gandhi, emerged, who was to become the symbol of India to the world. Gandhi, a lawyer of 49, had recently returned from South Africa where he had spent almost the whole of his adult life. There he had made his name as the leader of the Indian community in their fight against discrimination by the South African government, using his own method of protest which he called *Satyagraha* or "soul force" To draw suffering upon oneself and thus shame ones opponent into a change of heart, to die-but not to kill-for the truth. When Gandhi returned to India in 1915, he found his own country strange to him and spent a year or two travelling around, finding out what the people were thinking.

Gandhi

At that time, although his reputation had preceded him, his views had always been those of moderates, and no one had really considered him as either a spokesman or potential leader. He believed however that experiments in passive resistance in India had shown that there was a place for his kind of nonviolent approach to political action. Gandhi was right. His moral condemnation of the new security laws struck a chord in the hearts of all classes. By using religion he made the political movement acceptable to all the people of India. He proposed a traditional Hindu method of protest-the *hartal* a closing of all shops and places of business as a sign of mourning. All over India people responded to Gandhi's call. The Hartal in many places led to violent rioting. Horrified, Gandhi tried to call off the strike but it was like reasoning with a whirlwind, it merely grew more violent particularly in the Punjab. Thousands of demobilised soldiers had returned home with little hope of a future. The government of the Punjab, believing the 'hartal' to be merely a cloak for rebellion was determined to suppress any signs of revolt. The situation was ripe for an explosion. It took place on April 13, 1919 in the town of Amritsar.

Bal Gangadhar Tilak was a great Sanskrit scholar and astronomer. He fixed the origin and date of Rigvedic Aryans, which was highly acclaimed and universally accepted by orientalists of his time. His role in Congress and advocating Home Rule for India were enormous. His newspaper (Kesari) founded in 1881 is going strong even today. He was Guru to V.D. Savarkar and hundreds of nationalists and thousands of Indians. He led the Indian Freedom Movement, till 1920, his death. After him Gandhiji took over. Although Gandhi accepted Gokhale as his mentor, in practice, he adopted all of Tilak's ideas of Swadeshi and of social reform.

His words, "Swaraj is my birthright and I shall have it!" roused a sleeping nation to action, making Indian people aware of their political plight under a foreign rule. Tilak did not question the British Sovereignty nor his demands were rebellious or revolutionary. All he was asking was favourable conditions in India, to enable people to learn to govern themselves. May be all over the world, the separatist forces should follow his vision and define freedom as ability to govern one's land. But the handful rulers who ruled India's millions thought otherwise. They thought that Tilak was whipping a rebellion and he was imprisoned twice; two years for the first and six during the second. They said, he had committed treason.. Tilak rightly calculated the attitude of the British towards the economic exploitation of the Indians. The British used the raw material from the Indian soil and produced finished products in their country, which in turn were sold in India. This made the Indians totally dependent on the British. In the process, all the self-employing industries of India like spinning, weaving, glass making, sugar, dyeing, paper making were destroyed. People became destitute for no fault of theirs to help an empire become richer and stronger. To fight this situation, he gave four mantras called Chatuhsutri: (1). Boycott of foreign goods (2) National Education (3) Self Government (4) Swadeshi or self reliance. He realized that mere protest against British rule was not going to help and insisted on native production and reliance. He founded Deccan Education Society to give better education as per the country's needs. He wrote articles over inhuman punishment meted out to the nationalist youth who protested the division of Bengal (Vanga Bhanga). Indian newspapers were not to criticize the British policy in those days and two articles titled "Has the Government lost its head ?".and "To Rule is not to wreak vengeance" appearing in Kesari landed him in jail, after a namesake trial. For the first time in British history, intellectuals in England (including the great orientalist, Max Muller) were able to convince the Government that the trial was unfair. But the second time (1908) was no different. Tilak advocated his own case and when the judgment of six years of black-waters (kala pani) imprisonment was pronounced, he gave the famous statement :

> *"All I wish to say is that in spite of the verdict of the jury, I maintain my innocence. There are higher powers that rule the destiny of men and nations. It may be the will of Providence that the cause I represent may prosper by suffering than by remaining free".*

His trial and punishment led to national upheaval. But the British were careful enough to arrange everything in secret and the judgment was delivered at midnight and Tilak was taken under military vigil to be deported to Burma (present Myanmar, which was also under British control).

At 52, Tilak wrote his famous commentary on Bhagavad-Gita, the sacred book of Hindus; Gita-Rahasya in the jail. By the time Tilak completed his six year prison term, he was the unquestioned leader of the Indians-the uncrowned king. He was known as the Tilak Maharaj. There was unprecedented jubilation after Tilak was free and back in India.

Civil resistance, the concept of Swaraj, and nationalism had taken deep roots. Tilak's suffering did not go in vain. A band of leaders, full of zeal for nationalism and self-sacrifice was coming up. National schools were coming up in all corners of India. He paved the way for Khadi (hand woven cloth), picketing against foreign goods and alcoholism. His death in 1920 brought Mahatma Gandhi on the scene and Gandhiji gave a concrete shape to Tilak's ideas of Swadeshi.

DIFFERENCE FROM THE CONGRESS

Apart from firing up college students, educated Indians and people in the cities, the Leagues elicited little response or enthusiasm from India's masses and the British government. It was often divided upon whether to follow up with public demonstrations, or compromise by contesting elections to the legislative councils that were criticized as little more than *rubber stamps* for the Viceroy.

Its further growth and activity were stalled by the rise of Mohandas Gandhi and his *Satyagraha* art of revolution: nonviolent, but mass-based civil disobedience. Gandhi's Hindu lifestyle, mannerisms and immense respect for Indian culture and the common people of India made him immensely popular with India's common people. His victories in leading the farmers of Champaran, Bihar and Kheda, Gujarat against the British authorities on tax revolts made him a national hero. Gandhi realized that India was 900,000 villages, not the cities of Bombay, Delhi, Calcutta and Madras. Most of its people were poor, illiterate and farmers, not Western-educated lawyers.

Many Indian political leaders opposed Gandhi's ideas. These included Bal Gangadhar Tilak, Muhammad Ali Jinnah, Annie Besant, Bipin Chandra Pal and Lala Lajpat Rai, who scoffed at the notion or simply favoured negotiations and discussions with the British. But Gandhi's immense popularity with the people and the younger generation had transformed India's politics. He transformed the Indian National Congress from a body of educated Indians and city folk, to a 15 million strong organization spread across almost every province, town and village.

THE ARCTIC HOME

Tilak's other work is 'The Arctic Home' in the Vedas. While writing The Orion, he came across certain statements in the Vedic literature which led him to ponder over the problem of the original habitat of the Aryans. However, he could not find the leisure required for such a serious study in the political and social conflicts in which he was engaged at that time. But when he was imprisoned for sedition in 1898 he could devote his attention to this problem. It was at this time that Max Mueller, the greatest Vedicist had sent him a copy of the second edition of the Rigveda edited by him. It is interesting to note that Max Mueller had developed great respect for Tilak's scholarship although he did not agree with his theories. Actually the Oxford Professor pleaded for leniency for Tilak when he was imprisoned. He put his signature to a petition which urged consideration in respect of Tilak. He wrote:

> *"My interest in Tilak is certainly that of a Sanskrit scholar for though I do not agree with argument put forward in his `Orion' or `Researches into the Antiquity of the Vedas' (Bombay 1883), I cannot help feeling sorry that he should lose the benefit of his labours. I sent him the edition of my Rigveda, but I am told that he is not allowed to read even his Bible and Prayer-book in prison."*

Tilak conceded that he was released in twelve months because of the efforts of Max Mueller and others.

Tilak was deeply interested in the edition of the Rigveda which he received from Max Mueller. He was highly impressed by the statement 'suryodayat prak bahuni ahani asan' meaning 'many days have passed before the sunrise'. It was this statement that led him to trace the original home of the Aryans in the Arctic region. He wrote this book when he was involved in the Jagannath Maharaj adoption case. In the Orion, he had shown, on astronomical grounds, that the antiquity of the Vedas can be stretched back to 4500 B.C. Tilak says in the Preface to the Arctic Home, that it is a sequel to the Orion in which it was unmistakably pointed out that the vernal equinox was in the constellation of Mriga or Orion during the period when the Vedic hymns were composed, and that it had receded to the constellation of the Krittikas or the Pleiades (about 2500 B.C.) in the days of the Brahmans. The next logical step was to trace the original home of the Aryans.

Tilak began to ponder over the problem and was immersed in thinking about references to the sun, day, night, dawn and so on. He was very happy when he found the statement that many days have passed before the sunrise for it implied a very long day and a very long night. This phenomenon occurs only in the Polar region and the logical conclusion therefore was that the original home of the Aryans was in the area of North Pole. Although the climate in that region is extreme cold, a few studies had appeared in the latter half of the last century according to which it was mild in the Interglacial period when human habitation there was possible. This was established geologically and several scholars had therefore argued that the original home of the early man must be sought in the arctic region where the plant and animal life also originated. In fact one Dr. Warren of Boston University wrote a book entitled Paradise Found or the Cradle of the Human Race at the North Pole. Tilak very meticulously employed all scientific evidence very judiciously and developed his theory of the Arctic home of the Vedic Aryans, He argued as below.

1. According to the latest geological evidence, which cannot be lightly set aside, the last glacial period must have closed and the Post-Glacial commenced at about 10,000 years ago, or 8000 B.C. at the best, and the freshness of the Siberian fossil deposits favours this view.
2. There were at least two Glacial and one Inter-Glacial period, and the geographical distribution of land and water on the earth during the Inter Glacial period was quite different from what it is at present.

3. There were great vicissitudes of climate in the Pleistocene period, it being cold and inclement during the Glacial, and mild and temperate ill the Inter-Glacial period, even as far as the Polar regions.
4. There is enough evidence to show that the Arctic regions, both in Asia and Europe, were characterised in the Inter-Glacial period by cool summers and warm winters-a sort of what Herschel calls, a perpetual spring; and that places like Spitzbergen, where the sun goes below the horizon from November till March, were once the seat of luxuriant vegetation that grows at present, only in the temperate or the tropical climate.

It has been recently suggested that Tilak's view was influenced by the writings of Reuben Burrow who wrote on Hindu myths in 1789. He was of the opinion that the equator lay further to the north and that temperate climate once prevailed in Siberia. Polar regions had six months' light and six months' darkness and the sun shines in the North Pole continuously for six months. Tilak quotes Dr. Warren who in turn quoted Captain Pim,

"On the 16 March the sun rises, preceded by a long dawn of forty seven days, namely, from the 29 January, when the first glimmer of light appears. On the 25 of September the sun sets, and after a twilight of forty eight days, namely on the 13 November, darkness reigns supreme. so far as the sun is concerned, for seventy six days followed by one long period of light, the sun remaining above the horizon one hundred and ninety four days.

Bibliography

Alva, Joachim: *Leaders of India,* Bombay, Thacker & Co., Ltd., 1943

Arabinda Poddar : *Tagore : The Political Personality*, Kolkata, Indiana, 2004.

Atri, Ajit : *Gandhi's View of Legal Justice*, New Delhi, Deep and Deep Pub., 2007.

Bapat, S. V.: *Tilak Sukti Sangraha*, A Kesari Prakashan, Pune, 1926.

Barua, B. P.: *Raja Rammohun Roy and the New Learning*. Hyderabad, 1988.

Bhat, V. C.: *Lokmanya Tilak*, Prakash Publications, Pune, 1956.

Bhattacharya, Sabyasachi : *Vande Mataram : The Biography of a Song*, New Delhi, Penguin, 2003.

Butalia, Urvashi: *The Other Side of Silence*: *Voices from the Partition of India,* New Delhi, Penguin, 1998.

Campbell-Johnson, Alan: *Mission with Mountbatten*, London: Hale, 1982.

Chatterji, Joya: *Bengal Divided: Hindu Communalism and Partition, 1932-1947*, Cambridge, Cambridge UP, 1994.

Collier, Richard: *The Great Indian Mutiny*. New York, 1963.

Dabholkar, Kunda: *Bharatiya Stree Shikshan*, Joshi Lokanade Prakashan, Pune, 1973.

Dasgupta, Subrata : *The Bengal Renaissance : Identity and Creativity from Rammohun Roy to Rabindranath Tagore*, Delhi, Permanent Black, 2007.

Guha, Ramachandra : *India After Gandhi : The History of the World's Largest Democracy*, New Delhi, Picador, 2007.

Hasan, Mushirul: *India's Partition*: *Process, Strategy and Mobilization*, New Delhi, Oxford UP, 1993.

Heisner and Goldberg: *Tilak and the Struggle of Freedom*, Peoples Publishing House, New Delhi, 1956.

Kesari-Maratha: *Tilak Birth Centenary Number*, Pune, 1956.

Lohia, Ram Manohar: *Guilty Men of India's Partition*, Allahabad, Navahind, 1960.

Lumby, E. W. R.: *The Transfer of Power*, London, Allen, 1954.

Manto, Saadat Hasan: *Kingdom's End and Other Stories*, Delhi, Penguin, 1987.

Mathur, Y. B.: *Women's Education in India 1813-1966*, Asia Publishing House, 1973.

Nagendranath Chattopadhyaya: *Mahatma Raja Rammohan Rayer Jiban Charit,* Calcutta, 1881.

Pandey, B. N.: *The Break-up of British India*, London, Macmillan, 1969.

Phadke, Y. D.: *Shodh Bal-Gopalancha*, Shri Vidya Prakashan, Pune 1977.

Richard I. Cashman: *The Myth of the Lokamanya: Tilak and Mass Politics in Maharashtra,* Berkeley, 1975.

Samaddar, Ranabir: *Reflections on Partition in the East*, New Delhi, Vikas Publishing House, 1997.

Tinker, Hugh: *Experiment with Freedom, India and Pakistan 1947*, London, Oxford UP, 1967.

Index

❑❑❑